TABLE OF CONTENTS

Top 20 Test Taking Tips

1. Carefully follow all the test registration procedures
2. Know the test directions, duration, topics, question types, how many questions
3. Setup a flexible study schedule at least 3-4 weeks before test day
4. Study during the time of day you are most alert, relaxed, and stress free
5. Maximize your learning style; visual learner use visual study aids, auditory learner use auditory study aids
6. Focus on your weakest knowledge base
7. Find a study partner to review with and help clarify questions
8. Practice, practice, practice
9. Get a good night's sleep; don't try to cram the night before the test
10. Eat a well balanced meal
11. Know the exact physical location of the testing site; drive the route to the site prior to test day
12. Bring a set of ear plugs; the testing center could be noisy
13. Wear comfortable, loose fitting, layered clothing to the testing center; prepare for it to be either cold or hot during the test
14. Bring at least 2 current forms of ID to the testing center
15. Arrive to the test early; be prepared to wait and be patient
16. Eliminate the obviously wrong answer choices, then guess the first remaining choice
17. Pace yourself; don't rush, but keep working and move on if you get stuck
18. Maintain a positive attitude even if the test is going poorly
19. Keep your first answer unless you are positive it is wrong
20. Check your work, don't make a careless mistake

Enterprise-wide Deployment

Contributions of Philip B. Crosby and George D. Edwards to quality control

Philip B. Crosby is perhaps best known as the author of *Quality is Free*, one of the seminal texts of quality control. This book was extremely popular with American managers. It extolled the benefits of doing things right the first time. Crosby also is known for promoting his four cardinal rules of quality management: the performance standard should be set as zero defects; quality is the same thing as conformance to requirements; quality is achieved by preventing defects; and the measure of quality's value is the cost of nonconformance. George D. Edwards is known as the first president of the American Society for Quality. He was the head of the inspection engineering department for Bell Telephone Laboratories. He was instrumental in advancing their groundbreaking quality assurance program.

Contributions of W. Edwards Deming to quality control

W. Edwards Deming is known as one of the fathers of quality control. One of Deming's primary insights was his use of statistical methods to promote quality control. He also championed the distinction between common- and special-cause variation. His most widely known contributions to the field are the so-called "seven deadly diseases of the workplace" and "14 points for management." According to Deming, seven "deadly diseases" can afflict organizations. These "deadly diseases" include: a lack of consistency in planning; emphasis on short-term profits; poor performance evaluation systems; excess turnover among employees; overreliance on the metrics that are the easiest to obtain; excessive medical costs; and excessive liability costs, typically associated with legal departments. Deming argued that all of these problems can drain resources, personnel, and ultimately profits from a business, and they are even more insidious because often they go noticed.

<u>14 points for management</u>
Maintaining consistent purposes and adopting a new philosophy: W. Edwards Deming outlined fourteen points for management. These points are basic guidelines for the promotion of quality. The first point is that managers should maintain consistent purposes. These purposes should be to maintain high product or service standards, to be competitive in the marketplace, and to keep people employed. Deming was reacting to what he perceived as pervasive short-term thinking in the business world. He advocated the establishment of research and development programs enable constant innovation and progress within the organization. Deming's second point is that businesses must embrace whole-heartedly the new quality philosophy, including lobbying governments for laws that foster quality. Deming believed that the entire organization, from senior executives to new employees, had to believe in the merits of quality improvement programs. This point was in part fueled by nationalist sentiment during a period in which American businesses felt threatened by foreigners, particularly the Japanese.

Eliminating dependence on inspection and ceasing to award business based on price alone:
Deming's third point for management asserts that inspection should be eliminated as much as possible. In Deming's view, inspection programs are

ineffective because they spot mistakes only after they occur. He believed that setting up programs to stop mistakes before they happen is far better. In addition, inspection programs can be costly to establish and maintain. Deming said that businesses should spend this money on improving production processes. The fourth of Deming's points for management is that business should not be awarded solely because of price. Instead, businesses should create a measure of total cost and use this measure to make their buying decisions. As much as possible, businesses should have a single supplier for each part, product, or service, because this practice will enable them to monitor quality and establish beneficial relationships. Deming approved of long-term relationships with suppliers because these relationships create greater opportunities for customization and optimization. Also, he asserted that businesses would be better off in the long run if they purchased top-quality goods rather than goods that cost the least.

Constant quality improvement and on-the-job training: Deming's fifth point for management is that production and service systems should be improved continuously so costs can be decreased continuously. Constant quality improvement can be achieved only by unceasing attention to the desires of customers. Businesses always should be improving the methods by which they gather and use customer information. Customer desires change over time, so data collection never should cease. Deming distinguished continuous quality improvement from solving problems, which is an ineffective way to achieve constant improvement over the long run. Deming's sixth point for management is that all employees should receive on-the-job training. Employees should receive training in all areas that pertain to their work, and managers always should

understand the tasks of their subordinates. Effective training requires steady and productive communication between all layers of the organization. Also, training programs should be based on concrete and specific performance standards.

Establishing leadership and eliminating fear: The seventh of Deming's fourteen points for management is to establish effective leaders. The purpose of management should be to set a proper example rather than to monitor the behavior and performance of subordinates. If training is effective and standards are clear, employees should not need constant supervision. Managers always should do their jobs with an eye toward improving quality. In addition, managers should have the authority to resolve issues they observe in the workplace. The eighth of Deming's points for management is that fear should be eliminated as a source of motivation. Deming observed that many organizations terrorized their employees with the constant threat of demotion or firing. He felt that this was an ineffective way to inspire loyalty and quality. Moreover, employees should feel comfortable enough in their jobs to consider possible innovations or to raise questions with their superiors. Likewise, managers should not be afraid of receiving comments or complaints from their subordinates.

Reducing interdepartmental barriers and reducing pressure on the workforce: The ninth of Deming's fourteen points for management is the reduction of barriers between departments. Deming promoted interdepartmental communication as a method for reducing waste and improving quality in all areas. To some extent, employees need to be trained in all other departments. In complex organizations, of course, this practice is not always possible; nonetheless, at the very least

- 6 -

managers should be familiar with the tasks and responsibilities of the other departments. Deming observed that many businesses segmented their departments and evaluated performance as such, so departments in a failing business might appear to be thriving. To Deming, this seemed like an ineffective system. He was in favor of linking all departments together. The tenth of Deming's fourteen points for management is that workers should not be pressured with short-term production goals. Instead, workers should be encouraged to embrace a holistic, long-term program for quality improvement. Constant exhortations and work targets, in Deming's view, contribute to anxiety and lower production among workers. Goals never should be set for individual employees, but instead for larger groups.

Eliminating quotas and ineffective management styles: Deming's eleventh point for management is split into two parts. The first part is a declaration that production quotas should be eliminated. In many factories, managers establish concrete production goals. For Deming, this sort of leadership is ineffective because continuous improvement always will affect the appropriateness of targets. According to Deming, encouraging employee pride and promoting quality is more sensible and will generate better results than mere focus on quotas. In a more general sense, the second part of this point for management is managers' responsibility to avoid basing their decisions on short-term objectives. Deming believed establishing a positive long-term plan and adhering to this plan made more sense than pursuing immediate gratification in the form of quotas or sales targets. By emphasizing continuous quality improvement, managers create the conditions for success.

Promoting employee pride and emphasizing quality over production: The

twelfth of Deming's fourteen points for management is divided into two parts. The first part is the promotion of employee pride. Deming felt that employees will do a better job when they are given the chance to feel responsible for their work. Furthermore, he felt that businesses should look for opportunities to link employees with their work, such as giving employees control over over multiple tasks in production or service provision. Deming felt that fear and anxiety in the workplace were obstacles to employee pride and therefore to quality. Employees always should be taught to emphasize quality over numerical production. Indeed, the second part of the twelfth point for management is the promotion of quality over production. To Deming, this practice meant the abolition of merit systems, which reward success within the business rather than improvement of the business. Deming believed that rewarding employees for the volume rather than the quality of their work set up bad incentives. In other words, this improper emphasis would encourage employees to make decisions that harm quality.

Encouraging self-improvement and universal buy-in: Deming's thirteenth point for management is the creation of self-improvement programs. Deming believed that organizations thrive when employees feel that their personal goals align with the goals of the organization. One way to achieve this alignment is by helping employees better themselves through in-house education opportunities. Employees always should believe that effort and self-improvement can lead to promotion within the organization. The last of Deming's fourteen points for management is universal buy-in. Deming believed all members of an organization should subscribe to the new vision of quality improvement. Managers are responsible for informing and encouraging their subordinates. All the employees will not be able to adhere to the quality management program unless it is made plain that adherence will advance their own as well as the organization's interests. Moreover, Deming felt that managers always should be alert for opportunities to increase employee participation in quality improvement.

Contributions of Armand V. Feigenbaum to quality control

Armand V. Feigenbaum was an aggressive promoter of total quality management. He outlined four key actions businesses needed to take in order to implement TQM programs: establishing standards; measuring conformance to these standards; resolving issues hindering conformance; and continuously planning for improvement. Feigenbaum was also known for his Nine M's of quality: markets, management, men, money, motivation, materials, machines, modern information sources, and mounting product requirements. By *mounting*, Feigenbaum mean consistently improving. Feigenbaum was one of the first quality specialists to insist that quality standards be assessed from the perspective of the customer rather than the perspective of the business. He argued that all standards should pertain to qualities for which a customer would be willing to pay. In the past, businesses frequently ignored customer desires.

Contributions of Joseph M. Juran to quality control

Joseph M. Juran emphasized the idea that quality control always should be considered from the perspective of the customer. Juran advocated deep involvement by management in the process of quality improvement. His version of quality management had three main components. First, he advocated quality control and the use of statistical

control methods for the mitigation of problems. He also promoted quality improvement and the use of the breakthrough sequence for resolving persistent problems. Finally, Juran promoted quality planning, and in particular annual quality reviews for the purpose of enshrining quality control efforts. Walter A. Shewhart, meanwhile, combined economics, engineering, and statistics in his work. He is widely known as a top engineer at Western Electric and Bell Telephone Laboratories and as the author of *Economic Control of Quality of Manufactured Product*.

Contributions of Kaoru Ishikawa and Genichi Taguchi to quality control

Kaoru Ishikawa was one of the main promoters of total quality control in Japan, where the field would become wildly popular and even more sophisticated than it had been in the United States. Besides the diagram named for him, Ishikawa is credited with developing the quality circle, in which work groups rather than lone employees resolved problems. One of his most popular ideas was that employees should be involved as much as possible in quality management issues. Genichi Taguchi was another top advocate of quality management in Japan. He wrote *Design of Experiments*, which included the first signal-to-noise measurement. Taguchi was employed by Japan's Ministry of Public Health and Welfare, where he promoted the use of statistics in quality management.

Six Sigma

Six Sigma is a program for improving business processes. The name is derived from the Greek letter sigma, or σ, used in statistics to indicate the standard deviation for a particular set of data. The standard deviation suggests the amount of variation between the members of the data set. Statisticians describe variation in terms of units of standard deviation, or sigma units, in order to provide a more accurate picture. Imagine a process that can be represented graphically as a bell curve. The centerline of the process is a time of 25 minutes, meaning that this is the average time required to complete the process. If the standard deviation is 30 seconds, then six standard deviations, or 6σ, would be either 22 minutes or 28 minutes. The general intention of Six Sigma is to improve all business processes such that six standard deviations will fit between the mean and both the upper and lower acceptable limits.

Lean

Lean is a comprehensive system for decreasing waste and increasing cycle times and quality. The tools of lean (e.g. 5S, velocity, spaghetti diagrams, level loading, and process cycle efficiency), are used in every phase of DMAIC. Many of the ideas of lean date back to Henry Ford, but the credit for assembling and updating the system goes to Taiichi Ohno, an employee of Toyota in the 1970s. In Japan, the philosophy is called *muda*. The general strategy of lean is to identify activities that add value and activities that do not add value. As much as possible, lean businesses try to eliminate activities that do not add value. These judgments always are made from the perspective of the consumer. Lean methodology is very similar in this respect to Six Sigma.

Transparency, velocity, and value
The lean philosophy emphasizes three areas: transparency, velocity, and value. Transparency is easy access to useful information. A business has achieved transparency when processes can be observed and measured. Errors should be noticed immediately and rectified. Velocity, meanwhile, is the speed with which processes are completed. The

ultimate measure of velocity is the interval between a customer's order and the delivery of the good or service. In lean methodology, velocity is sometimes called flow. The goal of lean is to reduce process lead times and enable the business to respond quickly and agilely to customer requests. Finally, value is the set of qualities or characteristics for which a customer is willing to pay. The goal of lean is to increase value and diminish waste. Value always is assessed from the perspective of the customer.

Inventory
In lean methodology, inventory and work-in-progress are considered drags on progress rather than assets. A lean business will try to keep very little inventory on hand and instead will strive to respond quickly to customer orders without relying on the storage of works-in-progress. A general habit involves finishing work in progress before handling new orders, which slows down production. Lean emphasizes other strategies for improving velocity. For instance, business can find ways to increase the number of completions per hour or eliminate redundant or unnecessary process steps. A business could improve velocity by decreasing errors or waiting time. A business also could improve velocity by decreasing the necessity of moving resources or personnel. When velocity is increased through these strategies, value tends to increase as well.

Application of Six Sigma tools to a service or transactional process

While no single way describes the application of Six Sigma tools to service or transactional processes, several rough guidelines exist. First, a Six Sigma black belt and champion would take a distanced look at the organization to identify business needs. Finding critical customer needs that can be measured from a distance is important. The black belt and champion then would define the scope of a Six Sigma project and draft a project charter. The next step would be to identify the key process output variables (KPOVs) for the project metrics. At this point, the black belt and champion would identify a team of key stakeholders and conduct an initial meeting. They would discuss the problem statement, gap analysis, goal statement, and SIPOC diagram. The black belt then would meet with the finance department to discuss the business impact of the project and the financial metrics that should be used. They also would calculate the cost of poor quality (COPQ) and the cost of doing nothing different (CODND).

While the Six Sigma black belt is meeting with the finance department, the champion and the rest of the team can be determining the customer information required for the project. This group also could be identifying potentially useful secondary metrics. At this point many teams will find it a good idea to create a Gantt chart. Next, the black belt and team would begin compiling project metrics in a time series format with infrequent subgrouping or sampling. The team should create control charts or run charts for the key process output variables. In other Six Sigma projects, this time would prent the opportunity to concentrate on specifications. However, in service or transactional processes, considering long-term capability and performance metrics in either frequency of occurrence units or percentage beyond desired value is appropriate. These measures should be placed in financial terms and used as base-line performance. All of the nonconformance issues associated with this process should be placed on a Pareto chart.

After making a Pareto chart of all the nonconformance issues related to the process, the Six Sigma black belt and the rest of the team could create a detailed flowchart or process map and study it for possible areas of improvement. At this time, the team could implement some lean methodologies. The black belt and team then would draw up a cause-and-effect diagram to look for variables that affect outputs. This diagram can be assembled with the help of the process flowchart and Pareto chart. Next, the black belt and team could create a cause-and-effect matrix in which the relationships between input variables and key process output variables are considered. The data collected can be assessed with a measurement systems analysis, especially in situations where nonconformance issues may be classified incorrectly.

In a typical Six Sigma project related to a service or transactional process, the measurement systems analysis would be followed by the application of a Pareto chart to the cause-and-effect matrix. Specifically, the black belt and the rest of the Six Sigma team will use the Pareto chart to indicate the relative importance of the input variables identified by the matrix. The resulting Pareto chart will suggest the key process input variables (KPIVs). The next step will be to prepare a failure modes and effects analysis and evaluate the current control plans. The team then will make a plan for data collection and begin implementing some initial changes to the process. The collected data must bear on the suspected relationships between KPIVs and KPOVs. The team then will attempt to depict the sources of variability in forms such as box plots, marginal plots, and multi-vari charts. The statistical significance of relationships between KPIVs and KPOVs may be evaluated with hypothesis tests.

After using hypothesis tests to find the statistical significance of the relationships between KPIVs and KPOVs, the black belt leading a project based on a service or transactional process will decide whether to investigate output variability by performing variance components analysis. For example, the black belt might be interested in the differences between departments or times of day. Next, the black belt would oversee statistical studies related to the impact of KPIVs on KPOVs. These may include correlation and regression studies, analyses of variance, and analyses of means. The team then will implement another set of process improvements. At this point, the team will decide whether to perform designed experiments to test the possible impact of process change ideas. In many cases, these experiments will provide insight into the relationships between change ideas and noise factors.

After performing any advisable designed experiments, the black belt in charge of a service or transactional project will calculate the best operating windows of the key process input variables (KPIVs). The control plan will need to be updated at this point, and control charts should be implemented to identify special-cause variation related to KPIVs. The final tasks for the black belt and team are to confirm the process improvements, stability, and performance metrics. This confirmation should be done through targeted demonstration runs. At this point, the black belt should bring the Six Sigma champion and process owners back into the project. The entire Six Sigma team will create a final project report and indicate the financial benefits of the project. This complete report should be disseminated or at least made available throughout the organization. If possible, the results of the project should be applied to problems elsewhere in the business. Responsibility for the process should be returned to the process owner. Performance should be monitored at three and six months after the end of the project.

Applications of Six Sigma tools to a manufacturing process

A Six Sigma project related to a manufacturing process can take any number of forms, but all such projects feature a general trajectory. A typical manufacturing project will begin with a meeting between the black belt and champion. These two employees will take an extremely long-distance look at the organization, sometimes called a "satellite view," and identify a pressing business need. This need should be considered in terms of customer requirements. The black belt and champion will establish the project scope and draft the project charter. Next, they will identify the key process output variables (KPOVs) to be measured. The next step in the typical manufacturing project will be to identify the key stakeholders and conduct an initial meeting. The fledgling team will consider any issues likely to interfere with status reporting or the project schedule. At the initial meeting, the team, the champion, and the process owner will consider the problem and goal statements. They also will create a gap analysis of the process to customer needs and a SIPOC diagram.

After conducting the initial meeting, the black belt in charge of a manufacturing project will meet with the finance department to determine the monetary impact of the proposed project. The black belt and the finance department will agree on appropriate financial metrics for the project. They will also calculate the cost of poor quality (COPQ) and the cost of doing nothing different (CODND). After finishing with the finance department, the black belt will identify the customer data required for the project. The black belt also will define the secondary metrics such as rolled throughput yield. The black belt and team then will create a general project plan and perhaps create a Gantt chart for guidance. The black belt and team then will compose control or run charts for the key process output variables (KPOVs). These charts should be taken from a considerable distance, known in Six Sigma as the 30,000-foot level. A set of charts from this distance will obviate problems later in the project.

After drafting run and control charts from the 30,000-foot level, the black belt heading up a typical manufacturing project will lead the team in the identification of long-term process capability and performance metrics for the key process output variables. These metrics will be based on the aforementioned control charts. All of the relevant nonconformance issues can be organized on a Pareto chart. At this point, revising the costs of poor quality and doing nothing different may be necessary. The next step in the project will be to compose a process map or flowchart with enough specificity to indicate possible problems. Using lean manufacturing tools might be useful at this point. The next move will be to generate a cause-and-effect diagram that suggests the variables related to process output. The entries for this diagram may be based on the process flowchart and the Pareto chart of nonconformance issues.

After creating a cause-and-effect diagram of all the process input variables, a Six Sigma manufacturing project team will make a cause-and-effect matrix indicating the strength of the relationships between the process input and output variables. Next, the team will take a step back and perform a measurement systems analysis. This analysis tests the integrity of the collected data. Another approach is to assess the repeatability and reproducibility of the measurements with a variance components analysis. This latter analysis also will assess the variations between different machines. The team will then place the input variables from the cause-and-effect matrix on a Pareto chart. The Pareto chart should identify the possible key process input variables (KPIVs). Next, the team will prepare a targeted failure modes and effects analysis. In most cases, the FMEA should be from a systems perspective, and the input items should be the most important sources of variation identified by the cause-and-effect matrix. The team then will need to assess the current control plans and implement the first set of process improvements.

After implementing the first set of process improvements, the typical manufacturing project team will create a plan for data collection. They will begin to gather data related to the relationships between key process input and output variables (i.e., KPIVs and KPOVs). The next step is to represent graphically the sources of process variation. Some of the tools useful for this representation are multi-vari charts, box plots, and marginal plots. The black belt and team then can use hypothesis tests to determine the statistical significance of the relationships. It may be useful at this point to perform a variance components analysis related to the sources of output variability. In some instances, there will be variation based on the day of the week or the particular machine. The relationship between KPIVs and KPOVs is further explored though statistical studies such as regression and correlation analysis, analysis of variance, and analysis of means. After all of this analysis, the next batch of process improvements may be implemented.

After implementing the second batch of process improvements, the typical Six Sigma manufacturing project team will decide whether to conduct designed experiments and response surface analyses. In many projects, the experiments will be organized with the intention of making the process more robust with respect to raw material variability and other noise factors. The Six Sigma team then will use the results of designed experiments to identify the best operating windows for key process input variables (KPIVs). This task should suggest some process improvements, which then may be implemented. The team will then error-proof the key process inputs as much as possible and update the control plan. The typical manufacturing project team then will apply control charts from a moderate distance, known in Six Sigma as the fifty-foot level. These control charts are useful for identifying special causes of variation in key process input variables.

After the Six Sigma team has composed control charts from the fifty-foot level, they will set about confirming the process improvements, as well as the process stability, capability, and performance. All of these values should be obtained through demonstration runs. The team then will create a final project report outlining all of the benefits, especially the financial benefits, of the project. This project report should be made available to every member of the organization. The improvements made by the project might apply to other areas of the organization. After meeting with the process owner, the Six Sigma black belt and team gradually can divest themselves of responsibility for the process. However, the champion and black belt should monitor process performance at three and six months after completion of the project.

Kaizen philosophy

Kaizen is a Japanese philosophy that governs all aspects of business. In kaizen, constant efforts should improve the quality of the business. These improvements are continuous and subtle, unlike those produced by Western-style innovation. In kaizen, improvements are small and frequent. Many improvements are based on the insights and experiences of lower-level employees, in contrast to the Western business model, in which changes typically result from executive orders. The initial concern of the kaizen business is attracting and maintaining good employees. The kaizen philosophy asserts that good employees will make good processes inevitable. Kaizen can be successful only with adequate training, defined operating practices, and buy-in from all employees. Furthermore, in kaizen, constant communication exists between employees at all levels. Kaizen is one of the more effective systems of total quality management.

Flow, pull, and perfection
In the kaizen philosophy, flow is the quality of continuous process accomplishment. The goal of kaizen is to create continuous flow through the organization rather than improving limited areas of a process. When a process has good flow, materials and information do not wait between activities. Businesses tend to create inefficiencies when they focus only on flow in one or two areas. Instead, flow should be considered from the perspective of the entire business. Pull is another concept in kaizen. In this system, pull means that each activity in a process should receive only the necessary materials and resources when subsequent activities are demanding the process be completed. In other words, instead of pushing resources through the process chain, it is more effective to have them be drawn along by the vacancies created by completed projects down the line. Finally, in kaizen the term perfection is defined as the ultimate goal of continuous improvement. By eliminating waste and streamlining processes, an organization can approach perfection.

Events
Kaizen is a Japanese system of continuous process improvement. The intention of a

kaizen event is to implement quickly the continuous improvement strategy. This implementation usually takes between three and five days. The first step in a kaizen event is to train employees in the general principles of kaizen. The next step is to define the problem to be solved by this particular kaizen event and to frame the desired result in terms of a goal. Before progress can be made, the process as it currently exists must be measured. In some cases, the organization will realize during this stage that a sufficient measurement system never has been created for the process, in which case it may be necessary to devise one. This occurrence can extend the duration of the kaizen event. The next phase of a kaizen event is brainstorming, during which the participants generate possible solutions to the problem. All proposed solutions should indicate clearly the path from the present to the future state.

In the typical kaizen event, the next step after settling on a solution is implementation. As such, implementation can take a considerable amount of time, and results may not be definitive by the end of the event. However, the initial implementation may suggest some possible ways that the solution can be tweaked. Furthermore, a defined follow-up plan should define the method for making changes to the implemented process. After the solution has been implemented and a full cycle has passed, results should be gathered and presented to the rest of the company. The final stage of a kaizen event celebrating success. While this stage might sound trivial, it reinforces the value of the program and encourages similar projects in the future.

Lay-offs
In order for kaizen to work, employees must be committed fully. However, this commitment can occur only when management has established a few fundamentals. First, the company must have a strict and explicit policy regarding lay-offs caused by kaizen projects. Employees never should worry that their improvement efforts will result in personal job loss. Of course, continuous improvements will reduce the need for employees in some areas of the business. These employees should not be laid off; instead, they should instead be transferred to a kaizen department where they can contribute to subsequent projects. In most cases, the implementation of kaizen will lead to greater demand in the future, so these transferred employees eventually will be required. Kaizen and other lean techniques always aim at increasing productivity by liberating resources. If demand does not increase, the organization can continue to improve until attrition brings the number of employees in line with needs.

Effective kaizen culture
Managers must take specific steps to ensure that employees commit to continuous improvement. The first and most important of these steps is training every employee in the basics of kaizen. This training can be done during employee orientation or at the beginning of a kaizen event. Furthermore, managers must establish incentives for employee participation. Employees should be encouraged to make suggestions and contribute to the implementation of kaizen solutions. These incentives should be based on metrics related to employee performance rather than merely on results. In other words, employees should be rewarded based on their dedication to the kaizen program rather than the success of any particular improvement project. The incentives should be considered from the perspective of the employee. Finally, managers should give their employees chances to advance and accept more responsibility within the kaizen program. If employees view kaizen as a way to advance their own careers,

they will be more likely to give it their best effort.

Training for Six Sigma

In order for a Six Sigma program to take root, managers must allow their subordinates to take part in training activities. This course of action necessarily will remove employees from their normal duties. Managers should take the long view and realize that Six Sigma training will improve productivity in the future. Managers should be among those persons who introduce Six Sigma to their employees. Whenever possible, managers should attend or at least appear at Six Sigma training sessions in order to reinforce the endorsement. In addition, managers often have valuable insights into the customization of training for their employees. Managers should permit their employees to participate and take an active role in Six Sigma implementation. Once Six Sigma projects have been initiated, managers should establish metrics for the use and effectiveness of these projects.

Six Sigma deployment

Use of data

Six Sigma is driven by data in every phase, from deployment through execution. First, managers compare customer and internal data to find areas where processes are failing. Six Sigma always evaluates quality from the perspective of the customer, so reliable means of acquiring customer data are important. Critical-incident surveys are one of the best tools for this purpose. Another way to identify Six Sigma projects is statistical analysis of databases. An undirected database analysis looks for unexplained patterns, while a directed database analysis inspects a particular variable. An undirected statistical analysis may identify ultimately meaningless patterns, so any findings should be subjected to

designed experiments. The traditional source of ideas for Six Sigma projects is process data. This data is inexpensive to obtain, in part because usually it already is being generated. However, this data must be analyzed objectively in order for it to be useful.

Enabling measurement and feedback

A Six Sigma program cannot be effective unless employees can receive unmediated and candid feedback from customers. Moreover, customer feedback and process data must be communicated through appropriate, easy to understand metrics. In Six Sigma, metrics always should relate to factors critical to quality, cost, or schedule. As much as possible, metrics should result from collaboration between all the parties to the project. Universal participation is conducive to universal buy-in. In Six Sigma, efforts are aimed at improving performance after improvements, so each metric should have a time component. Also, metrics should be comprehensible immediately to employees at all levels of expertise. Six Sigma metrics should require no further processing. The representation of Six Sigma metrics often is called a dashboard, and indeed, it should be as easy to read and understand as the display panel in a car.

Managers leading by example

In Six Sigma, every employee has to buy into the program. For such wide-spread acceptance to be possible, managers must lead by example. They must consider their every word or act and its possible effects on employee participation. Managers must model the behaviors they want to cultivate in their employees. For instance, a manager always should be looking to train himself or herself in his or her areas of weakness. A manager can consider himself in the same manner that a process is considered in the theory of constraints: he should find his weakest skill and then work to improve it until it has reached a tolerable level. Managers should be firm in their decisions but still flexible and open to persuasion based on data. Managers never should be seen to place their own needs above the priorities of the group. Above all, managers should be team players and should convey to their employees that the organization is a cohesive organism in which every part is vital.

Resource allocation for Six Sigma projects

Resource allocation can be one of the trickiest parts of Six Sigma deployment. Managers unfamiliar with the benefits of a Six Sigma program may not want to excuse their subordinates for training and implementation exercises. It is very important to emphasize that Six Sigma will be remunerative in the near future. Moreover, once Six Sigma is installed and operational, it will require fewer resources. In an average Six Sigma organization, only about 1% of the workforce is black belts. These employees will work only on Six Sigma projects. In a smaller company, black belts may comprise a larger percentage of the total workforce but may spend some of their time on work unrelated to Six Sigma. Smaller companies also have the option of cross-training their employees so they may fill different Six Sigma roles for various projects.

Six Sigma champions

In Six Sigma, champions are managers who oversee projects and ensure the projects align with the broader strategic goals of the organization. Most companies initiate their Six Sigma program by selecting and training a set of champions. These champions in turn select the first batch of black belts. Some basic personal and professional requirements apply to champions. A champion, first, should be

energized by Six Sigma. The champions who introduce Six Sigma to the rest of the company's employees must be enthusiastic capable of transferring that enthusiasm. As a result, a Six Sigma champion must have charisma. He or she must possess respect within the organization. In addition, a champion should have the technical skills to supervise Six Sigma implementation. A champion should be able to align Six Sigma projects with customer desires. Champions should know how to represent Six Sigma projects in objective terms.

Appropriate training
Champions typically are the first members of an organization to be trained in Six Sigma, so it is especially important for their training to be effective. In most cases, the first step in champion training is a basic class lasting two or three days. The focus of this introductory course is the role of champions in building a Six Sigma program. Champion training always should include workshops in which participants are given the chance to practice some of the techniques they are learning. Part of the training should focus on the selection of black belt and green belt candidates. Another part should focus on the selection of appropriate projects. The majority of the training session, however, should be a crash course in the basics of Six Sigma. Aspiring champions should learn about the merits of the program, as well as about its differences with other systems of quality management and continuous improvement.

Six Sigma black belts

Six Sigma black belts are employees tasked with leading quality improvement projects. In most cases, black belts work full-time on Six Sigma projects. Black belts must be expert in all the technical areas of Six Sigma: statistical analysis, implementation, and measurement. Moreover, they must be charismatic and influential within the organization. Black belts must be effective communicators so they can build support for projects and give clear instructions to their team members. Black belts should be respected by the other members of the organization, and they should have the authority to carry out their mission. Finally, and from a personal standpoint, black belts need to be comfortable taking risks. Not every Six Sigma project will be an immediate success, and some projects may need massive revision. A Six Sigma black belt needs to be comfortable reacting to adverse conditions.

Appropriate training
Training black belts before green belts is preferable so the black belts can plan projects while the green belts are trained. Then, once the green belt training is complete, the projects can commence immediately. Another approach calls for combining green belt training with the first week of black belt training. The black belt curriculum can be organized such that the first week covers material relevant to service as a green belt as well. Combining training is one way to reduce the costs of implementing Six Sigma. The traditional schedule for black belt training was one week per month for four months. During the four-month stretch, participants are given ongoing assignments so they can apply what they have learned thus far. The advent of online Six Sigma training programs has made accelerated training possible. When businesses administer part of their training online, students can proceed at their own pace.

Participatory nature of training: Black belt training is not comprehensive unless it includes a complete practice project. Six Sigma is a process, not just a knowledge base, so it must be performed in order to be learned. Moreover, a practice project is not considered complete until the sponsor has closed it and the financial results have been confirmed by the accounting department. It is best to tailor the project to the specific strengths of the black belt: that is, the project should concern processes with which the black belt candidate already is familiar. In many training programs, prospective black belts are asked to compile a list of possible projects before training begins. These projects may be initiated during the early phases of training, so the data gathered can be used in workshops.

Six Sigma green belts

A green belt has a basic training in Six Sigma, such that he or she can participate in projects led by a black belt. A company typically has more green belts than black belts, and the green belts are spread throughout the organization, so green belts are associated with every process or business function. In most organizations, green belts do not spend all of their time on Six Sigma projects. Green belts are often technicians, clerical staff, and process supervisors. To succeed as a green belt, an employee needs to have a solid technical understanding of the targeted processes or functions. In addition, a green belt needs to be committed to the Six Sigma methodology. Green belts should be employees with whom the black belts will be comfortable working. They should be good communicators and respected by their colleagues.

Appropriate training
Green belt training covers the fundamentals of Six Sigma. Because the work of each green belt will be restricted to his or her areas of expertise, only the general outlines of Six Sigma methodology are addressed during training. Most companies only need a week to train green belts. The main intention of the training is to give green

- 17 -

belts the vocabulary and knowledge base to understand the instructions given by black belts during projects. Green belts also must learn how to work as part of a Six Sigma project team. One intention of green belt training is to acquaint the members of project teams with one another so they can settle into roles. Green belts do not need to understand the statistical analysis used in Six Sigma, although they do need to appreciate the utility of this analysis.

Leading projects

Some companies with well-established Six Sigma programs may decide to expand their program by allowing green belts to lead projects. This practice can be effective as long as the projects are chosen carefully. First, only green belts with project management experience should be allowed to head a team. These employees also should be skilled in statistical analysis, even if this skill was not acquired during Six Sigma training. To lead a team, a green belt must be allowed to ignore his or her other work responsibilities. Leading a Six Sigma team is too large and important a task to be performed part-time. A black belt always should be assigned to oversee green-belt-led projects so any errors can be corrected in real-time.

Expectations for project team members

Black belts are in charge of project teams, but they need the assistance of the team members in order for the project to succeed. A black belt should have certain reasonable expectations for the members of his or her project team. First, a black belt should expect that the members of the team will be committed to the avowed goals as well as to the plan for reaching those goals. Of course, the black belt is responsible for encouraging the buy-in, but by the time the project is initiated the black belt should be able to assume that

all team members are committed. Black belts should expect that team members will communicate with one another and with their leaders. This communication should take the form of regular written reports and participation in meetings. A black belt should be able to trust that team members will report any problems and raise any pertinent questions as soon as is practicable.

What project team members should expect from the presiding black belt

The members of a project team are responsible for following the leadership of the presiding black belt, but they may have certain expectations for the black belt's conduct. For instance, the team members may expect that the black belt will give them an opportunity to reach their potential and contribute to the team's success. Team members should expect regular information about the group's progress. Team members may expect to receive credit for their work and correction when they are wrong. A team member has a right to expect some latitude and freedom with regard to project work. Ostensibly, green belts and other team members are chosen because they have some expertise in the targeted process or function. They should be given the chance to use that expertise as they see fit.

Organizational Process Management and Measures

Critical-to-schedule metrics

Cycle time is the most common critical-to-schedule metric. Cycle time is the duration required for the completion of a defined process. It may be called delivery time, order processing time, or downtime. The improvement of critical-to-schedule issues begins with making the distinction between process steps that add value and process steps that do not add value. Six Sigma professionals often use process efficiency and velocity numbers to assess value added relative to cycle time. In most Six Sigma projects, cycle time is considered secondary to metrics related to quality or cost. A project that focuses exclusively on reducing cycle time is more likely to compromise quality. However, it can be useful to baseline quality and cost metrics and then work to reduce cycle time. This ensures that quality will not be affected by any time-saving adjustments.

Critical-to-cost metrics

Critical-to-cost metrics identify areas of a process that significantly raise the expense. Critical-to-cost metrics should include not only the typical cost of a task, but also the increased cost of errors in the performance of this task. The likelihood of an error should be included in the metric. For instance, the metric should consider how long it will take to redo or repair a product made incorrectly. If a lag time exists in a process, the critical-to-cost metrics should include the cost of keeping materials on hand. The effects of errors on cost tend to multiply as the product moves farther down the path. In other words, a mistake made in the design phase will be significantly less expensive to resolve than an error in the manufacturing phase. The amount of money required to align a product or service with quality baselines is known as the cost of quality.

Critical-to-quality metrics

One of the more common critical-to-quality metrics is yield, or the amount of completed product divided by the amount of product that began the process. Obviously, a business would like to have yield equal 1 (or 100%). The difference between perfection and reality is known as the scrap rate. If a process had a yield of 95%, the scrap rate would be 5%. Yield is a useful metric, although it does not indicate where in the process errors occurred. Also, yield does not distinguish those pieces of scrap that can still be salvaged. A slightly more advanced metric is throughput yield, or the average percentage of units with no defects. When multiple steps in a process are considered, Six Sigma teams use rolled throughput yield, which measures the expected quality level after several steps.

Benchmarking

Benchmarking is a system of industrial research. In essence, it is continuous comparison with other, similar businesses. The most common form of benchmarking is comparison with a competitor or industry leader. However, businesses also can obtain useful insights by benchmarking specific departments and processes against similar components of otherwise different businesses. Businesses use benchmarking as a way to create effective and realistic performance standards. One positive side effect of benchmarking is that it creates enthusiasm and belief in the goals of Six Sigma projects. The leaders of the process can point to other businesses as evidence that improvement projects are worthwhile. Benchmarking also provides evidence that change needs to occur in the first place. Sometimes, the process of benchmarking indicates specific improvements. However, businesses should avoid the trap of imitating their competitors. It is better to use benchmarking data as inspiration for changes that are appropriate and tailored to one's own business.

Teams

A benchmarking team typically consists of between three and six employees familiar with the targeted process. The members of this team should have different skills and areas of expertise. For instance, a benchmarking team should include individuals skilled in facilitation, process documentation, analysis, and business research. Benchmarking teams function best when roles are clear and explicit. Some projects are so large that more employees may be needed, but as a general rule, benchmarking teams of more than a dozen are ineffective. If including this many employees is necessary, it is a good idea to divide the team into subgroups. Benchmarking is recommended when a business suffers some sudden trauma such as the loss of a major customer. A business also may decide to benchmark when it notices that a competitor is vastly outperforming it in a particular area. Many businesses set the identification of benchmarking targets as a continuous process so employees always will generate ideas for these projects.

Internal benchmarking

Benchmarking programs are comprehensive if they include internal, competitive, and functional projects. Internal benchmarking is comparison between similar processes or departments within the organization. For instance, a business that operates multiple factories might compare their performance. One motivation for internal benchmarking is that it forces the business to develop appropriate performance metrics. It also ensures that similar departments and processes are being measured in the same way and that these measurement standards have been approved by management. Internal benchmarking often is applied to training programs because large businesses run several different types of programs for entry-level employees, managers, executives, etc. Internal benchmarking can be a useful activity for aligning the standards for these training programs.

Competitive benchmarking

Competitive benchmarking is comparison with rival businesses in the same field. A few different approaches exist in regard to competitive benchmarking. Some teams find that enough information exists in the public domain to indicate the best practices and performance standards of competitors. However, in some cases enlisting participation from the competitor is necessary. Such a situation can prove difficult. When requesting data for benchmarking, a team should focus on processes rather than outputs. For instance, a business might request information about cycle time, but it should avoid asking about profits or number of products sold. Most businesses are wary about giving out the latter sorts of data. In hypercompetitive industries, cooperative benchmarking can be very difficult. One solution is a joint program administered by a third party. In this model, each competitor receives data from the other(s) and can perform its own benchmarking.

Functional benchmarking

Functional benchmarking is a specific comparison with a similar process in another business that might otherwise be quite different. Businesses perform functional benchmarking when they want to improve performance in a very narrow area. For instance, a grocery store might benchmark its trucking department against a shipping company so it can learn new ways to speed up deliveries. Functional benchmarking entails identifying best practices and then creating a list of companies that perform well in these areas. One of the advantages of functional benchmarking concerns the possibility of creating quite a long list of possible targets and selecting only those targets for which comprehensive metrics are available. It is recommended that a team begin with a list of a hundred possible businesses and then pursue four or five of these ideas aggressively.

Collaborative benchmarking
Collaborative benchmarking is a cooperative information-sharing program involving at least two businesses. Collaborative benchmarking has many advantages, one of which is that it makes accurate data easy to obtain. When businesses collaborate on a benchmarking program, they can agree to measurement systems and ensure fruitful results of data collection. Of course, in order for collaborative benchmarking to work, all participants must have incentives. The projects often are initiated when non-competing businesses appear headed in a similar direction or when such businesses both perform a similar process. Partners in a collaborative benchmarking program often host employees from the other business, allowing them to observe processes and ask questions on site. Collaborative benchmarking can be very successful as long as the participating businesses communicate well and extend similar benefits to one another.

Planning phase
Benchmarking is divided into five phases: planning, analysis, integration, action, and maturity. In the planning phase, the target of the process must be defined. Something cannot be benchmarked unless it can be measured. The best metrics are related to outputs. Without metrics, objective comparison is impossible. The second objective of the planning phase is to identify the other business against which the benchmarking business will be compared. Obviously, the best businesses to benchmark against are industry leaders or businesses with a reputation for quality and efficiency. The final objective of the initial phase is to plan the process. First, the benchmarking team must find good sources of information about the other business. A business library is an excellent place to begin this search. In addition, a wealth of information about other businesses can be found on the internet. As the benchmarking team begins to collect data, it should be alert for other good sources.

Analysis and integration phases of benchmarking
The second and third phases of benchmarking are analysis and integration, respectively. In the analysis phase, the benchmarking team makes a comprehensive account of the practices being considered. Before a true and fair comparison can be made, subject mastery is important. Internal practices then can be compared with the best practices of other companies. Many teams also will use the data they have collected to predict future performance both for themselves and for the other business. This data usage can be useful in promoting improvement projects because it indicates how the failure to adjust will have adverse consequences in the future. The projection of future performance also suggests the range of possible improvement. In the integration phase of benchmarking, the team will adjust their goals and meet with upper management. At this point, the team should be able to give a good summary of the results and recommendations derived from the benchmarking process. The team should

be able to propose specific changes to business plans and procedures.

Action and maturity phases of benchmarking

The fourth and fifth phases of benchmarking are action and maturity, respectively. In the action phase, the business implements the changes inspired by benchmarking. These changes should not just be implemented, of course; they must be fine-tuned and tested to ensure that they have been applied appropriately. In the last phase of benchmarking, maturity, the team assesses whether the prior four phases have led to positive changes. A benchmarking project only concludes when the best practices for the targeted process are in line or ahead of industry standards. Also, benchmarking should include recommendations for continuous improvement, as it may be assumed that competitors will also be improving their processes. Indeed, it may be incorrect to describe the "conclusion" of benchmarking, since similar processes must be ongoing to maintain competitive advantage.

Scorecards in performance measurement

Scorecards are a common tool for measuring performance. They break performance down into a series of categories, each of which is assigned a few top-level metrics. The most typical version, known as the balanced scorecard, contains four categories: financial, customer, internal, and innovation. The customer metrics should be based on satisfaction, while the internal metrics should relate to those aspects of company performance most closely aligned with quality. The innovation dimension, sometimes called "learning and growth," should feature metrics of how much the business is working to stay current and improve its processes, products, and services. The balanced scorecard gives a quick, comprehensive look at the organization's performance. Some critics, however, charge that the balanced is an overly simplistic view and does little to suggest possible areas for improvement.

KPIs

Key performance indicators (KPIs) are metrics monitored by the entire organization to ensure that a strategic plan is being followed. Key performance indicators show the degree to which the business has achieved its goals, or at least the progress made. They indicate when continuous improvement programs are successful or need to be adjusted. Also, key performance indicators provide context for regular meetings between management and employees. KPIs make it possible for every member of the business to understand whether performance is acceptable. A key performance indicator should be tied directly to strategic goals. Of course, strategic goals must be written such that they can be objectively assessed. KPIs should relate to customer desires, whether those customers are internal and external. KPIs should be somewhat easy to obtain. Finally, they should be able to identify waste and inefficiency.

Product performance and performance on quality improvement

Certain key performance indicators commonly identify when a business is adhering to its strategic plan. Product performance metrics supply data about the features and functions of products. This data should be objective and should include all of the product's features and functions. Performance on quality improvement is a metric used by businesses that run a number of different strategic plans at the same time. The performance on quality improvement metric indicates the number of projects completed and ongoing; the financial

- 22 -

results; and the employees involved in each of these efforts. The financial results of quality improvement projects include the amounts gained, the amounts invested, and the return on investment. The performance on quality improvement metric enables a business to compare projects that may be quite different.

Competitive quality and the cost of poor quality

Competitive quality metrics focus on the aspects of performance that influence product sales. These aspects could include the speed of transactions, the degree to which customers are pleased with service, and the accuracy of order fulfillment. In some industries, competitive quality metrics will indicate the extent to which the delivered product meets the expectations of the consumer. Some of this information must be obtained directly from customers, which means the business may need to solicit or pay for it. The cost of poor quality metric is the gap between current costs and the costs that would be incurred without any waste, error, or inefficiency. The cost of poor quality gives a business a target and a motivation for improvement efforts. Of course, the precise value of the cost of poor quality cannot be known. Most businesses develop programs for estimating the cost of poor quality in the most significant areas.

Performance of business processes and product and process deficiencies

Performance of business processes metrics only recently have been refined to the point that they can be used as key performance indicators. In most organizations, business processes are so large and disparate that they are difficult to measure. Businesses should establish internal standards for cycle time, errors, and other relevant values. Another tricky KPI is product and process deficiency. These are represented in a manner similar to cost of poor quality. For

instance, a business might determine the cost of poor quality for every hour of work or for every shipped product. These values contribute to the overall picture of the cost of poor quality, which itself can be difficult to calculate. Generating values for product and process deficiencies is important because these values can be compared between products and departments.

Customer satisfaction and customer loyalty

Customer satisfaction and customer loyalty are related but not identical. A satisfied customer may still buy from a competitor if he or she believes that the competitor offers better value. A loyal customer, on the other hand, will be more likely to buy from one company and ignore offers from competitors. Loyalty is more difficult for a business to engender than satisfaction. Satisfaction may be indicated by what customers say, but loyalty is indicated by what they do. A company should try to cultivate loyal customers and should reward loyalty as much as possible. When a customer is loyal, sales are more stable and the business can spend less money trying to throw a net over the entire market. Customer satisfaction can be measured only in single encounters, while customer loyalty can be assessed over a long interval.

Financial impact of customer loyalty

Businesses prize customer loyalty because they know it translates into hefty financial benefits. One way to calculate the financial impact of loyal customers is to determine the net present value of the profits over a certain interval. In other words, the economic value of the loyal customer is the current value of the money that customer will spend over the approximate period of loyalty. This period is expanded or contracted depending on the industry. Some industries, such as

- 23 -

automotives and computers, are more fertile ground for customer loyalty. Companies also consider the retention and defection rates for their customers. The retention rate is the percentage of customers who make repeated purchases, while the defection rate is the percentage who make one purchase and then take their business to a competitor. Research has shown that the defection rate and profits are inversely correlated; that is, as one goes up the other goes down, and vice versa.

Financial measures

Revenue growth, market share, and margin

Revenue growth indicates the change in sales figures over time. Essentially, revenue is the money that a business brings in through its operations. If revenue is growing, then the business should have more money to reinvest and make capital improvements. Of course, growth in revenue can be offset by growth in expenses. Market share, meanwhile, is the portion of a given market services by a business. Market share provides information about the level of competition in a market, but it does not necessarily indicate whether a business is serving the market efficiently. A business may believe that because it holds a large market share it does not need to continue working to serve its customers. Finally, margin is the amount of money a business needs to create in order to sustain operations. Obviously, businesses want to earn profits far in excess of the margin, but they also should consider whether profits are being reinvested effectively in order to create the conditions for long-term growth.

Cost of quality, net present value, return on investment

Cost of quality is a measure of the financial resources required to create a good product or service. Businesses isolate those costs that directly influence the quality of their work and focus on these costs in their reinvestment and capital improvement strategies. Although higher quality generally entails higher cost, continuous attention to the specific factors that influence quality can result in lower costs without the sacrifice of quality. Net present value is the difference between the current worth of cash inflows and the current worth of cash outflows. This measure is used in investment decisions. If the money expected in the future from an investment is greater than the money required at present, the investment is a good idea. Finally, return on investment is the money recouped after an initial outlay. Businesses keep track of ROI to determine whether capital improvements and investments have been wise.

Cost-benefit analysis

Cost-benefit analysis is a rigorous evaluation of the consequences of a business decision. It attempts to simply decision-making by weighing the possible positive consequences of a decision with the burdens created by it. Businesses perform cost-benefit analysis before purchasing equipment, introducing new products, or hiring new employees. A comprehensive cost-benefit analysis will include not only the immediate consequences but also the second- and third-level consequences of a decision. A full cost-benefit analysis has three components: a preliminary survey, a feasibility study, and a final report. In the preliminary survey, the team gathers information about the decision. The feasibility study estimates the degree to which the idea will fulfill the requirements of customers. Finally, the final report presents the team's findings. The cost-benefit analysis may be stopped at any point if it is determined that the negative consequences outweigh the positive.

Team Management

Team formation

Successful Six Sigma teams usually do not cooperate without conflict at the beginning. Indeed, most groups must pass through some conflict and reconciliation periods before they can work effectively. The trajectory of a team has been codified according to four stages: forming, storming, norming, and performing. In the forming stage, the members of the team are getting to know one another, and so for the most part they are on their best behavior. At this point, the team has not yet begun working seriously enough to inspire much conflict. In the second stage, storming, the team begins its work in earnest, and differences between the members begin to emerge. During this stage team members will begin to assume different roles. The team leader must exercise control during this stage so conflicts can be resolved beneficially. In the norming stage, the team members settle their differences and settle on compromises that make effective work possible. This stage is called "norming" because team members are agreeing to normative behavior for the group. In the performing stage, the team operates at an optimal level because members have learned to work together.

Team leader

A team leader is responsible for establishing and maintaining protocol, the set of rules by which the team will operate. The team leader also is charged with continuously realigning the team's efforts with the original goals and objectives. A team often will need to review first principles in order to stay on track. A team leader also is responsible for handling any conflicts that should arise during the project. A team leader will be responsible for planning and administrating the team's meetings. The team leader must meet with stakeholders and project sponsors in order to keep them apprised of the group's progress. A team leader must work continuously to improve the team's performance, first by helping members brainstorm and then by refining solutions through the use of data analysis.

Common problems and solutions for teams

Team dynamics can be rough, especially during the early stages of a Six Sigma project. In order for a team to thrive, the roles must be defined and appropriate. In some cases, roles will be assigned by the team leader. At other times, it will be better for team members to settle into roles as they become familiar with one another. This latter process usually entails some conflict at first. A team also will struggle if members are not held accountable for their actions. Accountability is the responsibility of the team leader. Teams should meet only when necessary but should stay in regular communication throughout a project. When meetings do occur, they often are hijacked by members who digress, go off on tangents, or rudely reject the ideas of others. This behavior should be stopped immediately by the team leader. A similar group problem is groupthink, in which the members of a team are reluctant to disagree or do not have enough experience to come up with alternate solutions. Groupthink can result from having too little expertise in a team.

Handling overbearing group members

Hierarchies exist within a Six Sigma team, and sometimes senior members can run roughshod over their subordinates. Besides being rude, however, this behavior is bad for the team because it

- 25 -

alienates people and makes them less likely to share their ideas or commit fully to their work. When appropriate for one member of the team to have authority, such as when the team is dealing with that member's area of expertise, the black belt should allow that member some extra power. However, the black belt must make sure that this dynamic does not extend into other areas of the project. Moreover, the black belt must never let any team member assert him or herself without the support of data. Expertise and determination are necessary qualities in Six Sigma, but they cannot be allowed to crowd out cooperation and communication.

Handling dominant team members

An ideal Six Sigma team will contain driven, confident stakeholders. However, some team members will overstep these boundaries and begin to dominate their peers to the detriment of the team. If some members of the group talk too much, talk too much about themselves, or otherwise monopolize conversation, the black belt and other team members may need to intervene. Specific techniques can reduce the potential for dominant team members. For instance, some black belts apply nominal group technique, in which a vote determines the priority of agenda items. Another way to reduce domination by one group member is by subtly deflecting this behavior as it emerges. The black belt might ask the dominant team member to work individually on a separate part of the project or might redirect conversation.

Handling reluctant team members

For a Six Sigma project to be successful, every team member must feel comfortable sharing his or her ideas and opinions. It can be a problem when shy team members never contribute to group discussions. There always will be

introverted and quiet people, however, so there must be structures for eliciting their feedback. One easy way to enact such structures is for the black belt or meeting leader to question each member of the team directly during each meeting. These questions should be concrete and impossible to evade. It could be useful to give the shy team members a specific brief, which they are required to discuss at every meeting. The individual differences between team members should be respected, but they cannot be allowed to disrupt honest communication or the generation of good ideas from all members of the group.

Resolving feuds within a team

Every Six Sigma team contains a range of personalities, some of which inevitably will come into conflict. In many cases, the members of a Six Sigma team will have worked on the same process or in the same department for a long time and will have long-standing disagreements. This behavior is extremely counterproductive to the goals of the team and must be rooted out as soon as detected. Various approaches exist in regard to conflict resolution, such as arbitration, counseling, and peer mediation. Usually these problems should be handled by someone outside the team, since any intervention by a team member could be seen as taking sides. If the conflicting team members are essential to the success of the project and their dispute appears irreconcilable, they should be separated as much as possible. The black belt also should monitor this situation closely and should have individual consultations with all parties concerned throughout the course of the project.

Avoiding discounting participation by team members

Every member of a Six Sigma team is selected because they have unique and necessary skills. For this reason, every team member should feel that his or her insights and ideas are valued. The black belt or project leader should avoid situations in which a team member feels that his or her contributions have been discounted. Such situations can happen in a direct way, such as when a team member's suggestions or ideas are rudely dismissed by other participants. It also can happen more subtly, such as when a team member's contributions are ignored or passed over without comment. Of course, irrelevant or unuseful ideas and opinions always will present challenges to the progress of a team. The response to such comments should not denigrate the speaker, however. Instead, the black belt should try to foster an environment in which team members gently can indicate why a particular idea won't work. Not only does this response show respect to the speaker, it gives him or her some extra insight into the project.

Avoiding attributing negative motives to other people

In a Six Sigma project team, poor communication has a compounding effect: when team members fail to interact honestly, they begin to misunderstand each other and then communication becomes even worse. If team members begin to attribute negative motives to one another, the effect on the team can be poisonous. The black belt or project leader always should be on the alert for this type of behavior. Whenever a team member makes assumptions about why another person is doing or not doing something, these assumptions are symptoms of poor communication. The response should be to call a meeting and address the nature of the disagreement. Team members should be responsible for explaining the reasons for their actions to colleagues. Six Sigma is an empirical, fact-based discipline, and this emphasis extends to the interactions among team

members. The members of a Six Sigma team always should confirm the reasons for decisions and as much as possible should base their actions on information available to every member of the team.

Keeping groups from floundering

Despite the specific protocol for moving through Six Sigma projects, many teams have a hard time getting started or finishing. Different reasons can cause this trouble, depending on when it occurs in the project. If the team has trouble getting started, often they are unsure of the scope or purpose of their efforts. Such a sense of uncertainty indicates that the black belt and sponsor have done a poor job of composing or publicizing the project charter. In such instances, the black belt should intervene and ensure that all team members understand what they are about to begin. If a team flounders in the middle of the project, usually data has been analyzed insufficiently, so the appropriate path forward is not evident to all team members. If the team flounders at the end of the project, effective contingency plans for making adjustments likely have not been conceived.

Avoiding the rush to accomplishment

Six Sigma is a program for success, but it does not produce instant results. Too often, team members are impatient during the course of a project, and they make mistakes in their rush to accomplishment. To keep this from happening, a black belt needs to be conservative when establishing the preliminary schedule. It is tempting to think that a team can be unprecedentedly fast and efficient, but setting unrealistic expectations can destroy morale. The success of a Six Sigma program relies on strict adherence to protocol, and the only way to ensure this adherence is to maintain a close watch on team members. Although checklists generally are not used in Six Sigma, they can be a good way to make sure that every step is taken on the road to project completion. When the black belt senses that a strong hunger for success among the members of the team, he or she may assign those members some easy tasks to provide that feeling of accomplishment.

Reducing unfocused conversation and digressions

One common problem in business meetings is inefficient conversational habits such as digressions or tangents. The black belt is responsible for ensuring that team communication remains focused and controlled. Every meeting should follow a strict agenda and should adhere to time constraints. Making a meeting open-ended is an invitation to time-wasting. In some cases, it is useful to set time limits for each item on the agenda. The black belt may want to designate some other team member as the time-keeper during meetings, since the black belt most likely will be busy with other matters. The time-keeper should have the authority to interrupt conversation and remind the team members of the agenda. However, sometimes unexpected issues will arise, and the black belt should be prepared to adjust the established time limits if fruitful conversation is occurring.

Effective change agents and issues that diminish buy-in from stakeholders

Most people claim to embrace change, but few people actually do so. Employees typically are reluctant to give up their old habits. To be effective change agents, the members of a Six Sigma team must first acknowledge the importance of having all employees on board with changes. Change agents take conscious steps to increase buy-in, commitment, and participation. Buy-in may be lacking if the goals of the project are unclear.

Employees are more likely to participate and conform when they see how the proposed solutions will benefit them personally. However, employees will be skeptical if they believe the project team has prejudices and preconceived solutions. If the project team does not communicate regularly with the employees, the employees will lose faith in the project. Finally, buy-in will be reduced if the project's goals are too diffuse. Having a number of small projects with single targets is better than one giant project with several targets.

Responses to conflict

Avoidance
Five basic responses to conflict exist. These responses include avoidance, accommodation, competition, collaboration, and compromise. Avoidance is the least cooperative and assertive way to resolve a conflict. If a person notices a conflict but fails to bring it up or pursue it, he or she is avoiding the conflict. This may seem an ineffective behavior in the business world, but in some situations, avoidance is the correct response to conflict. If the conflict is insignificant or the outcome is assured, avoidance may be the best approach. In other words, if there is no chance of getting one's way, it may be better to avoid a conflict. Avoidance may also be the correct response if tempers are already hot over some other issue. It may be preferable to avoid a conflict until the members of the team have settled down. Another time to avoid conflict is when the possible consequences of disagreement vastly outweigh the benefits of resolution. Finally, a team member may be justified in avoiding conflict if he or she feels other members of the team can do a better job of resolving the issue.

Accommodation
Accommodation is the suppression of one's own interests in order to serve the

interests of another person may be served. Accommodation can be a valuable tool in conflict resolution, as long as it does not engender resentment. In some cases, it team members should accommodate one another. For instance, a team member always should accommodate if he or she recognizes personal error. Another time to accommodate is when the issue is clearly much more important to the other person. When an issue is trivial to one person in a disagreement, that person may be better off conceding the point and hoping for consideration in the future. Accommodation also is appropriate when the group is fragile and more conflict could be very damaging. Of course, excessive accommodation can inspire some members to dominate the team, and in some cases accommodation will lead the team to accept the incorrect solution.

Competition

One response to conflict is competition, wherein the conflicting parties do their best to win. As long as the competition is fair, it can be a great way to settle disputes and generate excellent work. Most people perform better when they feel they are up against a competitor. Competition can be as simple as civilized argument during a meeting. Using competition as a response to conflict is appropriate when some members of the team are undecided. A team member also should be ready to compete when an issue is vital to the success of the business. Competition is an appropriate response to conflicts that need a clear resolution. An objective form of competition settles a dispute for good. When competition is used to settle disputes, the team leader should ensure that team members are fair and nice to one another. Also, competition sometimes becomes a habit in a team, which can be detrimental to cooperation in the future.

Collaboration

Collaboration is the response to conflict wherein team members work together to find a solution. When two team members disagree, they may collaborate until they come up with a resolution they both support. Collaboration is an effective style of conflict resolution when both parties have good points. Collaboration also is appropriate when members of a team have different areas of expertise, and so it is a good idea to combine their perspectives. Collaboration works when the conflicting parties have some personal disharmony; the process of collaborating may help them work through these problems. Collaboration also is a good idea when cooperation will increase buy-in from other team members and stakeholders. One problem with collaboration is that it can take a long time. For this reason, it should not be used to resolve unimportant conflicts. Also, collaboration can make room for too many viewpoints, which is a problem when some members of the team are inexpert.

Compromise

Compromise is a useful response to conflict when maintaining team harmony is more important than coming up with the best possible solution. Compromise, therefore, is not the right approach to ending crucial conflicts. It is appropriate, however, when two important members of the group are diametrically opposed on a key issue. If neither of these parties will give ground, a compromise may be the only way for the group to move forward. Compromise also can be the best course when no time exists for a lengthy debate or collaboration. Compromises can be very successful, but they sometimes leave the participants with lingering regrets. Also, compromises may produce mish-mash solutions that fail in the long run. Some problems require a clear, unified approach, and cannot be resolved through compromise. Finally, compromise should be avoided when it will disillusion some members of the team.

NGT

Nominal group technique (NGT) is a system for ranking non-objective data and is used primarily to create consensus or agreement in groups. Nominal group technique is used most commonly during the define and analyze stages of DMAIC. In the define stage, it is used to simplify project loads by combining redundant projects and eliminating unnecessary projects. In the analyze stage, nominal group technique helps teams agree on which solutions should be pursued. The first step in nominal group technique is to distribute paper to each team member. In the event of more than 35 options, each team member should receive eight pieces of paper; if there are 20 to 35 options, each member should receive six pieces of paper; and if there are less than 20 options, each member should receive four pieces of paper. Following discussion, each team member will select one option for each piece of paper he or she has received and indicate the option's rank on the paper. Then the papers are collected, and the weighted rankings are tabulated. The group then can focus on the most important and preferred options.

Affinity diagrams

Affinity diagrams organize a collection of issues, problems, or ideas so they may be utilized effectively. The diagram is so called because it identifies the affinities, or similarities, between seemingly disparate ideas or problems. Organizations using affinity diagrams often discover unforeseen relationships between variables. These diagrams often are used at the beginning of a process, when the team is trying to gain a primary understanding of the problem. An affinity diagram can be useful for building a consensus when members of a team have divergent interests and knowledge bases. However, affinity diagrams may be used in every phase of the DMAIC process. One common result of an affinity diagram is the identification and elimination of redundancies in thinking.

Creation
To create an affinity diagram, teams begin by identifying the target issue or problem. The next step is to have each member of the team list a few issues that impact this target. It is important to collect as many ideas as possible. Once the ideas are collected into a general list, they can be organized into categories. Redundant items may be discarded. Discussion or even argument about the logic of sorting is typical. The team leader should administer this part of the process calmly and proactively. Once the categories have been labeled and filled, the group should come up with header cards for each title. The titles may be useful for nominal group technique or in the creation of a prioritization matrix. If the process is a success, then the main ideas listed on the header cards will indicate the most important drivers to be addressed for the achievement of objectives and goals. It should be noted that affinity diagrams do not require objective information; instead, these diagrams are tools for organizing the subjective impressions of team members.

Process decision program charts

Process decision program charts (PDPCs) break a process down into its component tasks, with special emphasis on potential problems and solutions. As such, these charts are a useful tool for brainstorming protocols for handling crises that emerge during processes. Process decision program charts are used during the analyze and improve stages of DMAIC. In the analyze stage, they are effective for identifying the underlying causes of recurrent problems. In the improve stage, they may be effective at linking possible problems with probable solutions, so contingency plans can reinforce process. The top of the chart will name the process, and below this top line the chart will list the steps required to complete the task. These steps are presented in order from right to left. Below each step, one or two sub-steps may be necessary. However, it is recommended that the chart be kept simple. Under each step or sub-step, the chart should list some potential problems. Provisional solutions should accompany each of these possible problems.

Matrix diagrams

Matrix diagrams indicate the relationships between several items in multiple groups. A matrix diagram is a table in which the value in each cell indicates the strength of the relationship. Matrix diagrams often are used during the define and improve stages of DMAIC. In the define stage, these diagrams are used to pick projects that will contribute to the achievement of organizational objectives and goals. Also, matrix diagrams can be used in the define and improve stages to examine the similarity between customer desires and process metrics. The first step in the creation of a matrix diagram is to identify the items for comparison. Six Sigma teams often transfer the categories from some other chart, such as an affinity diagram. The next step is to use consensus decision-making rules to evaluate the relationships between each pair of values. In this subjective process, the team should perform carefully and according to an organized protocol.

A few different types of matrix diagrams exist, each of which may be useful in particular circumstances. In a directional system, arrows suggest the nature of the relationship between each pair of items. Sophisticated directional systems have weighted arrows that indicate the direction of causation as well as the importance. In a numerical matrix diagram, numbers perform the same functions as weighted arrows. For example, on a ten-point scale a 5 might indicate a moderate relationship in one direction, while a 1/5 indicates a moderate relationship in the opposite direction. In a plus-minus system, a plus sign indicates a relationship and a minus sign indicates the absence of a relationship. In a symbol system, finally, triangles, circles, and squares indicate characteristics of each relationship. Matrix diagrams typically have final rows and columns that tally up the total importance of each item or process. The team then can identify the items and processes that have the most significance.

Prioritization matrix

A prioritization matrix ranks choices. This tool is used primarily to build consensus in a group setting. Six Sigma teams typically use one of two methods for creating a prioritization matrix: either the full analytical method or the consensus-criteria method. Prioritization matrices primarily are used during the define and improve stages of DMAIC. In the define stage, prioritization matrices are used to help groups pick the projects most important to the organizational objectives and goals. A prioritization matrix can be an effective tool for comparing customer desires with process also metrics. As much as possible, a business wants to measure the qualities of a process or product important to clients. In the improve stage, a prioritization matrix can be used to confirm the alignment of projects with customer requirements.

Full analytical method of creation
The full analytical method of creating a prioritization matrix begins by listing options and the criteria required to evaluate those options. It Phrasing the criteria as targets such as lower cost or

greater employee satisfaction is important In the full analytical method, the first matrix contains comparisons of every criterion with every other criterion. Six Sigma teams typically use a numerical rating system in which 10 indicates the most importance, 1 the average level of importance, and 1/10 the least importance. In the second matrix, each option then is evaluated with respect to each criterion. Each option receives a final score compiled of his or scores on the weighted criteria. Most statistical software programs provide a summary matrix in which all of the options are ranked.

Consensus-criteria method of creation
When there are too many criteria or options or too little time to create a prioritization matrix according to the full analytical method, the consensus-criteria method can be a useful alternative. In this method, the initial matrix is discarded, and the team simply distributes a hundred points across the criteria in accordance with perceived importance. This method is slightly more subjective in its assessment of importance, but it is far less time-consuming. After the criteria have been weighted, they are compared with the options. The final score for each option is calculated by multiplying its score for each criterion by that criterion's weight. The larger the product, the more important the option. Both the full analytical and consensus-criteria methods of creating a prioritization matrix make an essentially subjective exercise into something a bit more structured.

Define

Obtaining customer information

Areas businesses tend to ignore
Many businesses pride themselves on their aggressive outreach to customers but fail to gather information about non-customers. Businesses should be concerned with the characteristics of people who choose not to buy their products, so they can consider how to appeal to these people. Businesses also should develop ways to identify customers who switch to a competitor but do not make a complaint or give any other alert of their defection. Sometimes, customers will switch to a competitor not because they dislike any aspect of their original purchase but because the competitor makes a special offer. A business should identify product features that cause customers to defect. Businesses also should develop ways to obtain information about customers who become dissatisfied with a product after its warranty period is over. These customers often see no point in contacting the manufacturer, who then loses a valuable source of information about customer desires and product failures.

Comment cards and formal surveys
Many businesses rely on comment cards and formal surveys for information about how customers view the business' products and/or services. The most basic metric obtained in these ways is customer satisfaction, and more specifically, how customer satisfaction is affected by various characteristics. Comment cards are left in places where customers will be, and customers voluntarily complete them. For this reason, very satisfied and very dissatisfied customers are overrepresented, because they are more likely to be motivated enough to fill out a card. A formal survey will attempt to gather information from a more representative sample of customers, although these surveys are often returned by the same highly motivated customers. Surveys are more effective when they ask customers for specific information about their preferences.

Focus groups
A focus group answers questions about the services or products of a business. The members of a focus group may be customers or non-customers. They may be a random group of citizens or members of a target demographic. Sometimes, businesses assemble focus groups of people from demographics in which they do particularly well or particularly poorly, in the hopes of learning the secrets of their success or failure. The typical format of a focus group is for the attendees to be presented with a sample of the product and then asked to give their impressions. The focus group will be more valuable when more specific and targeted information is obtained. In most cases, the members of a focus group will be compensated, but the leaders should make it clear that participants are to be honest. Focus groups provide direct insight into customer perceptions, but they are more expensive than other methods of obtaining customer information.

Field intelligence
Field intelligence is the information obtained by employees through their normal interactions with customers. For instance, a salesperson will gain insights into the desires of customers without ever asking a direct question. Any employee who talks or works with customers will pick up valuable information. The key for a business is to establish and maintain channels for this information. Open lines of communication must exist so field intelligence can reach

- 33 -

the higher levels of the organization. Some businesses establish mechanisms for gathering extra field intelligence. For instance, a retail store might set up video cameras in order to facilitate study of customer behavior. The store might be able to identify those areas where customers are more likely to linger.

Customer service and complaint management

Many businesses obtain most of their information about customers from routine customer service and complaint management. Executives in Six Sigma businesses commonly meet with customers personally. Some businesses establish programs in which every employee spends a certain amount of time dealing with customers. This practice prevents employees from pursuing goals that are distant from the concerns of the customer. Six Sigma businesses pay special attention to customer complaints. Any reports of error or malfunction are assessed and organized so pervasive problems can be noted. A good company makes it easy for customers to complainand for these complaints to be heard. Complaints are an excellent source of ideas for new Six Sigma projects.

Customer survey questions

For a customer survey to be useful, it must draw responses from a range of customers. Both satisfied and unsatisfied customers should be included. Survey questions should be designed to elicit useful responses. In other words, questions should be specific enough to generate actionable suggestions. The questions should be written at the level of the respondent and should not include any technical jargon. Every question should be pertinent. Questions should be designed to elicit an unbiased response; that is, questions should not lead the customer toward any particular response.

Survey questions should be ordered logically so the customer will not be confused. Many surveys are improved through the use of objective response measuressuch as the Likert scale, in which the respondent is read a statement and asked whether he or she strongly agrees, agrees, disagrees, strongly disagrees, or has no opinion.

Customer requirements in business-to-business transactions

In a business-to-business transaction, the buyer usually is very specific about product or service requirements. Typically the customer expresses a nominal value, or target, accompanied by upper and lower specifications. In other words, the customer declares the value he or she would prefer and then indicates the range of values he or she would tolerate. Any delivered products that fall outside this range are defective and will be returned. Defective products create waste for the customer and the supplier, alike. A supplier who consistently delivers defective products soon will be replaced. However, suppliers should not focus exclusively on the specification values expressed by customers, as such a focus gives a warped view of the customer's requirements. Instead, the supplier should focuson meeting the customer's stated requirements and looking for ways to add more value.

Customer requirements in business-to-customer transactions

In business-to-customer (B2C) transactions, the business usually has less information about the customer requirements than in a B2B transaction. Moreover, significant variations in customer requirements may exist. Some customers may have different requirements depending on other factors such as time of day or physical location. Collecting information about customers in

B2C transactions is time consuming and potentially expensive, but it gives the business the opportunity to micro-target market segments. That is, a business can take the information it gathers to develop small-scale marketing strategies for specific customers and potential customers. In a B2C transaction, customer requirements may not be expressed directly or explicitly. However, they may be just as objective and susceptible to appeal as those of a customer in a B2B transaction.

QFD

Quality function deployment, typically called by the initials QFD, is a system for ensuring that customer requirements are aligned with product and process requirements. Quality function deployment most often is used in the analyze and improve stages of DMAIC. In these stages, QFD is used to plot strategies for fulfilling customer requirements. The basic process of quality function deployment is to establish customer requirements, known as whats, and design requirements, known as hows. The customer requirements are what needs to be achieved, and the design requirements are how they will be achieved. A number of tables are used to assess the importance and significance of various design requirements in the promotion of customer requirements. If a customer requirement, or what, has very few or no design requirements, or hows, then improving the process may be possible. When there are hows without whats, the process may contain some non-value-added activities that can be eliminated.

Customer satisfaction and quality

Many business customers provide a range of tolerated specifications, but the supplying business errs if it assumes that providing a product within this range will maximize customer satisfaction. A customer may accept any product within the range and yet be more satisfied with products closer to the nominal (target) value. The Kano model is a chart with quality on the x-axis and satisfaction on the y-axis. As quality increases, so does satisfaction. A basic level of quality ultimately will leave the customer unsatisfied. A customer becomes more satisfied when the level of quality is exciting. However, the standard for exciting quality is constantly rising, as competitive pressures lead to technological advances that make previously acceptable products and services seem obsolete. The intention of the Kano model is to shift the focus from customer requirements to customer needs. The model underscores that businesses continually must innovate to meet the rising expectations of their customers.

Project charter

A project charter is an overview of the project. It changes as the project moves along, so team members and sponsors will remain on the same page. Management should approve the project charter in order to give the project legitimacy and informed guidance. A good project charter will establish clear deliverables, so its success or failure can be measured. Also, a good project charter will direct employee efforts to the right areas because it will identify the key variables that affect performance at all levels. A project charter will ensure that a proposed project does not interfere with other work performed in the company, because it will make public the intentions of the team. The project charter also will ensure that Six Sigma efforts are directed to the most important aspects of performance, and that they deal with processes integral to the business in the future.

Project statement, scope, and deliverables

The project charter is a document in which the most important details about the project are codified. Of course, this document will be subject to revision as necessary. One of the hallmarks of the DMAIC structure, and indeed of Six Sigma itself, is a willingness to rethink first principles at any time. The first step in composing an effective project charter is to make the problem statement explicit. The team should ask itself why the project is necessary. The reasons clearly should be integral to the optimal function of the business. Indeed, a project charter should express deliverable in terms of actual output and in a manner approved by the financial department of the organization. In most cases, it is necessary to confirm the reasonableness of the estimate with the finance department before writing it into the charter. The charter also should include a reasonable estimation of the project scope, based on the data collected thus far.

Schedule, stakeholders, and team composition

A project charter must include a provisional schedule. This schedule should include specific dates on which established objectives and goals are to be met. Although the schedule established at the beginning of a project is unlikely to survive the imposition of unforeseen events, project leaders should be as specific and prudent as possible. The project charter also should include a complete identification of the stakeholders in a project. Stakeholders are those persons who influence a project or are affected by a project. Along with an identification of the stakeholders, a project charter should include a list of the team members. Of course, the list of stakeholders and team members will feature significant overlap.

Finalizing a project charter

A project charter should include an appointment for an initial meeting, at which the team members will discuss and consent to the scope, deliverables, and provisional schedule to be included in the charter. This meeting allows team members to become acquainted with one another if they are not already and to voice any initial concerns or ideas related to the project. Having agreed upon the core items of the project, the team should map the top level of the process to be improved. This information should be entered into a new, updated version of the charter, which then should be submitted to the sponsor for approval. Obtaining this approval is important so both project participants and sponsors understand the nature of the work about to be undertaken. This way, any initial misgivings can be addressed without much loss of resources.

Problem statement

A project charter typically will begin with a problem statement in which the author defines an adverse situation in the business, or the target of the proposed project. If possible, a problem statement should provide measurable evidence of the problem's existence. It also should describe the problem in terms of poor outputs. The collection of objective data related to the problem may not be easy, particularly if the problem relates to a new business process or a process previously not addressed. However, the project charter should include as much preliminary data as possible, with the understanding that it will be updated as the project moves along and more data becomes available. The measure stage of the DMAIC model is an opportunity for the team to refine its charter through direct acquisition of data. The presence of objective data is important because it justifies the decision to direct resources toward the project.

Defining the business need

A project charter needs to identify the specific business need or needs that will be addressed by the proposed project. In other words, the charter must name the business processes that will be improved by the successful completion of the project. As with the problem statement, this section of the charter should include as much objective data as possible. It may be difficult for the author to estimate the value of the project to specific business processes, particularly if this estimate is based on minimal and preliminary data in the problem statement. However, if possible the charter should refer to specific metrics such as the number of defects, schedule, or profit. Many Six Sigma theorists recommend that all projects have a clear and measurable benefit to the customer. Comprehensive project charters will address business needs related to the customer, stakeholders, and other employees.

Statement of objective and identification of resources

A complete project charter should include a statement of objective in which the author provides a definition for the intended result of the project. Most Six Sigma experts recommend expressing this result in financial terms, since such terms are easy to understand and unlikely to vary. Other measures, like defects per million or return on investment, may be used but are more subject to variation and unforeseen influences. A complete project charter also will identify the resources required for the project. The efforts and time of the team members are not included in this summary. The resources may include equipment, materials, computer time, databases, and other employees. The resources required by a project are not only those resources necessary to improve the process, but also those necessary to collect and analyze data along the way.

Project scope

A project charter will include a clear description of the project scope, or the particular part of the problem to be targeted. For a number of reasons, it is better for projects to have a limited scope. Otherwise, objectives can become team members can become disgruntled, and resources can be wasted when a project stretches out indefinitely. In general, Six Sigma projects should take no more than four months. Longer projects run the risk of losing key members. If the members of a team have a vision that cannot be realized within four months, they should consider whether the grand project might be divided into multiple smaller projects. Indeed, the composition of the charter is an excellent time to consider the appropriate scale for team efforts. Often, a team will decide to solve a particular problem, only to discover that it depends on a collection of smaller problems that must be resolved first. In such a case, the team may want to conduct a series of smaller projects rather than grouping the entire problem in one project.

Sponsors

A project charter must identify the project's sponsors, or the managers who will provide guidance. The sponsors will provide funding to the project, give the team members access to resources, and inform other managers about the project's existence and intentions. One of the sponsor's jobs is to create enthusiasm and support for the project, so the project will receive any possible assistance from other employeesAs a result, the charter should identify appropriate sponsors. The sponsors should be selected from the departments most relevant to the project. In cases where the project participants are drawn from a number of different departments, the sponsors may need to be drawn from the ranks of those managers who oversee multiple departments. Such selection will make it possible for the project team to receive all the required support. Also, team members should avoid selecting sponsors who are already involved in several other projects.

Stakeholders and team members
A project charter should identify the stakeholders as clearly as possible. Stakeholders are all of the people and groups affected by the problem being addressed and potentially affected by the project as it progresses. In Six Sigma, the team should use a top-level process map to identify all of the affected groups. Affected groups may include customers, suppliers, other employees, and specific departments within the organization. The charter also should identify the members of the project team, or all the stakeholders participating in the project. Most projects are headed up by a single black belt, with one or more green belts representing each relevant department. Some projects may require the participation of experts or skilled employees. In rare cases, a Six Sigma project team will include a facilitator to ensure that all members of the team work together effectively.

Deliverables
A project charter should include a clear and measurable identification of the deliverables created by the project. A deliverable is any fungible benefit or advantage. Identifying deliverables is important because it enables the overall success or failure of the project to be assessed. Establishing targets for deliverables allows the project to be judged on its own terms. One common mistake is to list aspects of the project's method as deliverables. For instance, some project charters will identify the data obtained during the project as a deliverable. This is misguided, in part because the data would not be necessary if not for the existence of the project. Although systems such as statistical process control have utility for an organization beyond the scope of the

project in which they are created, they should not be counted as deliverables. If possible, deliverables should be placed in financial terms.

Schedule
A project charter should include some form of schedule, even if the schedule likely will be modified once the project begins. The schedule should include the date on which the charter was approved by the sponsor as well as the start and completion dates. A good charter will indicate the dates on which each phase of the DMAIC schedule will be complete. This process is known as a phase-gate review. The authors of the charter will use critical path or program evaluation and review technique (PERT) analysis to set the target dates. The schedule typically is expressed as a Gantt chart, in which each phase of the project is defined, and the prerequisites and required resources are listed. Each of the phases of the DMAIC schedule should be subdivided into a set of activities.

Objectives of the define stage

The method for problem solving in Six Sigma is expressed as the acronym DMAIC, which stands for define, measure, analyze, improve, and control. The first state, define, focuses on identifying and articulating a project's important characteristics, including identification of the goals, objectives, and scope of the project. The Six Sigma team also should make explicit the team members and sponsors, as well as the proposed schedule for the project. The Six Sigma team should define the desired result of the project, otherwise known as the deliverable. In considering the process to be improved, the team should identify the stakeholders, the input/output structure, and the functions involved. The other component of the define stage is selecting and assembling a team able to accomplish all of the proposed goals. The members of

- 38 -

this team must be able to work together well and must all have a solid understanding of the task before them. Moreover, all the members of the team should agree with the desirability of successfully completing the project.

Project status report

Project status reports begin with a current schedule and brief description of the project. A project status report should include a list of the action items, or the tasks to be completed by assigned team members at particular times. The project status report also will include lists of roadblocks, or hindrances to progress not yet resolvable by specific actions. A project status report also will include a list of the data obtained during each phase of the project. Finally, the project status report should list any items that should have been finished but have not yet. These are called outstanding items. Project status reports typically are issued once or twice a week and every time one of the DMAIC phases is completed. Copies of the report are sent to the sponsor, team members, and any other relevant stakeholders.

Gantt charts

Gantt charts are used to identify the critical path of each dependent task in a particular project. The critical path includes everything that has to be done to maintain the project's timing. Any process not on the critical path may be slightly delayed without extending the overall duration of the project. These activities are said to have built-in slack time. At the beginning of a Six Sigma project, distinguishing the tasks that are on the critical path is important. The use of Gantt charts typically is restricted to the define stage of DMAIC. The intention of this chart is to identify those tasks that, if truncated, would lead to an overall cycle time reduction. In addition, a

comprehensive Gantt chart will make it possible to place all project activities on the schedule. In some cases, a Gantt chart may be used during the improve stage to confirm the reduction of critical path cycle time.

Creation
Gantt charts are useful for identifying the critical path of a process. The first step in the creation of a Gantt chart is to make a list of all the tasks that have to be completed in the project. After these tasks have been placed in the order in which they need to be performed, it should be determined whether some tasks may be performed simultaneously or whether some tasks require the completion of previous steps before they may be initiated. On a Gantt chart, jobs that can be done at the same time are placed on parallel paths, and other jobs are placed in sequence. Within each parallel path, there may be serial tasks. However, if one of the parallel paths can be completed more quickly than another, then some slack time can be built in to that path.

Interpretation of Gantt charts
Gantt charts help businesses create the fastest-possible schedule for a process. The most important benefit of a Gantt chart is that it indicates areas within the process that can tolerate lag. Essentially, a process that is not on the critical path may be initiated a little late or finished a little early. For every task, though, there will be some time by which it must be initiated and some time by which it must be finished. Of course, it is not always possible to obtain a precise measure for the duration of a particular task. For this task, it may be necessary to perform program evaluation and review techniques (PERT) analysis. PERT analysis can gauge the probability of a task being completed within a certain amount of time.

Toll-gate reviews

A toll-gate review is a point of evaluation in a Six Sigma project. In a toll-gate review, all of the team members gather and discuss the success or failure of the tasks just completed. As such, this review offers opportunity to consider whether the objectives laid out in the planning stage have been accomplished. Typically a toll-gate review occurs at the end of every phase in the DMAIC or DMADV process. In most cases, the black belt conducts the toll-gate review, although all the other team members should participate. Toll-gate reviews typically involve the use of check sheets, project deliverables documents, and milestone lists. The toll-gate review should run according to an established structure and should be rigorous in its judgments. In the long run, there is no value in allowing a project to continue past the toll-gate review when the objectives have not been met.

Measure

SIPOC

SIPOC (suppliers, inputs, processes, outputs, and customers) analysis provides a comprehensive look at a process. SIPOC is used during the define stage of DMAIC, when the Six Sigma team tries to identify each top-level process, as well as its stakeholders. In the context of SIPOC analysis, suppliers are those persons who contribute inputs to the process. Inputs are defined as all of the knowledge, resources, and information required to produce the desired output. A process is defined as any task that translates inputs into outputs. Accordingly, the outputs are the deliverables, or the products of the process. Finally, the customers are all of those parties that receive the deliverables (outputs). SIPOC is initiated with the creation of a flowchart or process map. Typically, the first category to be identified is the outputs. From there, locating the customers, inputs, and suppliers will be easier.

Process cycle efficiency metric

The measurement of process cycle efficiency is used to determine the most useful and positive ways to improve cycle time. The process cycle efficiency metric is used most often during the analyze stage of DMAIC. The general method for calculating process cycle efficiency is to divide value-added time by process lead time. Process lead time is calculated by dividing the number of items in a process by the number of times the process is completed in an hour. This calculation is known as Little's law. A process can attain a maximum process cycle efficiency of 100% if all the activities in the process add value. However, it is more typical for processes to approach 25% efficiency after the implementation of lean strategies. The reasonable value for efficiency depends in large part on the type of activity. Creative activities usually have efficiency values of approximately 5%, although lean management strategies have been known to increase this figure up to almost 25%. Transactional activities, on the other hand, sometimes can reach efficiency values of up to 50%.

Value stream mapping

Value stream mapping is a communication tool for Six Sigma professionals. It depicts the flow of materials and information through an organization. Most value stream maps have two versions: a current state and a future state. The future state map depicts the process after planned improvements have been made. Ideally, the future state version of the value stream map will be less complicated than the current state. Value stream maps are effective when they identify waste and redundancy in processes. Each activity in a process should be represented with a shape on the map. Furthermore, each activity should be accompanied by the following information: cycle time, down time, in-process inventory, path of information, and path of materials. After a current state value map has been produced, it should be examined for steps that do not add value. These steps should be eliminated or minimized.

Process maps

Process maps are clear, easy to understand depictions of the sequence of steps necessary to finish a process. One common use for process maps is to identify the amount and type of value added at each step in the process. Process maps may be used during all of the stages of DMAIC. In the define stage, they are used to record top-level processes. In the measure stage, they are used to record the lower process levels and reveal differences in the perceptions of shareholders. During the analyze stage, process maps are used to investigate the sources of variation or excessive cycle time. In particular, process maps are good at finding process complexities, shareholders, and inefficient locations. Process maps often are used during the control stage to tell shareholders about change proposals. During the control stage, process maps may be used to record process adjustments.

<u>Creation and interpretation</u>
On a process map, a symbol represents every step in a process. Although it is possible to use the entire set of ANSI symbols for flowcharts, it is more common simply to depict decisions with diamonds and other tasks with rectangles. All decisions should be framed as binary; that is, only two possible answers exist. In more sophisticated process maps, shading or shaping will indicate delays or measurement intervals. As with flowcharts, one of the clearest signs of inefficiency on a process map is a glut of decision points. The goal of process maps is to spot redundant, unnecessary decisions and tasks and to discover ways to simplify processes.

Flowcharts

A flowchart is a basic tool for recording all of the steps in a particular process. Flowcharts are used during the measure, analyze, improve, and control stages of DMAIC. In the measure stage, flowcharts can be used to map a process as it is currently being performed or to identify how different shareholders perceive a particular process or problem. In the analyze stage, a flowchart can be used to identify complications in a process that can lengthen cycle time or cause adverse variations. In the improve stage, flowcharts can be used to diagram

possible improvements and changes. Finally, in the control stage, flowcharts can be used to map out processes that have been revised and improved.

<u>Creation and interpretation</u>
Flowcharts simplify communication by representing each task in a sequence with a symbol. Most organizations endorse the use of the symbols created by the American National Standards Institute. Some employees already will be familiar with the ANSI system, in which decisions are represented by diamonds and processes are represented by rectangles. Some flowcharts will incorporate different colors to suggest departmental divisions and time distinctions. Flowcharts are fairly easy to interpret, assuming the team already is familiar with the process. One thing to look for is a preponderance of decision points, as this occurrence may lead to unnecessary delays or adverse variations. The goal of process improvement is to reduce complications and unnecessary lags. Therefore, the interpretation of a flowchart always should be performed with an eye toward simplifying as much as possible.

Spaghetti diagrams

Spaghetti diagrams depict the movement of resources, materials, or personnel throughout an organization. Spaghetti diagrams are used during the analyze stage of DMAIC. These kinds of diagrams isolate wasteful movement, whether in regard to people or resources. The first step in the creation of a spaghetti diagram is to generate a map or floor plan of the relevant area. The site where the process begins is marked with a 1. The next destination for the person or material is marked with a 2, and a line is drawn between the 1 and 2. This process continues for the entire path of the person or material. Including landmarks and obstacles such as furniture and doors in the diagram is a good idea. Once the diagram is complete, it can be scoured for opportunities at simplification.

Attributes data

Attributes data indicates the number of times something occurs or appears in a sample. In Six Sigma, recording the number of errors in a process is common. This recording is known as attributes data. Attributes data is distinct from measurement data because it only indicates when something occurs: it does not indicate the degree to which it occurs. The attributes data associated with errors, for instance, would not indicate the degree of variation from specifications. Therefore, identifying when a problem is getting worse or better can be difficult. Also, attributes data does not always provide information useful for making decisions in the future. Whenever possible, Six Sigma professionals obtain measurement data. However, in some situations attribute data is sufficient.

Sampling methods

Various approaches to sampling exist. Simple random sampling occurs when every unit in the population has the same chance of being selected. When the population is divided into groups and a sample is taken from each of the groups, stratified sampling has occurred. In a systematic sampling program, some method exists regarding the selection of samples. For instance, every third unit might be selected. In a cluster sampling program, a representative group is selected out of the population, and then a random sample is drawn from that group. This method depends on the ability of the sampler to select a truly representative group. Finally, judgment sampling programs rely on expert opinions in their selection of a sample group. This mode of sampling is appropriate when the samples must have particular

characteristics not common to every member of the population.

Gauge repeatability and reproducibility analysis

Gauge repeatability and reproducibility analysis assigns a numerical value to the errors caused by a particular measurement system. Gauge repeatability and reproducibility analysis is used most often during the measure and control stages of DMAIC. In the measure stage, this analysis generally is used to assess the degree to which measurement error contributes to common- and special-cause variation in estimates of process baseline. It also can be used in this stage to confirm gauge discrimination. In the control stage, gauge repeatability and reproducibility analysis is used to evaluate the accuracy of specific measurement systems. The success of an R & R analysis depends on the collection of representative samples. A measurement system cannot be evaluated correctly except by its performance with respect to typical samples.

<u>Process</u>
When analyzing gauge repeatability and reproducibility (R & R), using samples obtained during actual operations is essential. Also, each appraiser should receive the samples in a random order, although someone other than the appraiser should be able to identify the samples. In a standard gauge repeatability and reproducibility analysis, there are three appraisers and ten samples: each appraiser measures each sample three times. However the test is arranged, there should be multiple trials for each sample in order for repeatability to be assessed. While a large sample size is preferable, this analysis can be expensive, which is a limiting factor. Again, it is essential to obtain a representative sample so all the potential sources of variation in the process are evident.

Interpretation of discrimination ratios and gauge repeatability and reproducibility

In gauge repeatability and reproducibility analysis, the discrimination ratio is an estimate of the number of different categories a measurement system can identify. In most cases, eight distinct categories are necessary before the measurement system can be subjected to statistical analysis. The gauge repeatability and reproducibility statistic typically is expressed as a percentage of total process variation or as a percentage of tolerance. If reported as a percentage of process variation, it suggests how useful the measurement system will be in process capability analysis and control charting. If reported as a percentage of tolerance, it suggests how useful the process will be for determining the acceptability of the process deliverables. If the measurement system error is large relative to tolerance, there is a greater chance of improperly accepting or rejecting output. For both tolerance and process variation, a percentage from 0 to 10% is acceptable, while a percentage of more than 30% is unacceptable.

Linearity analysis

Linearity analysis judges the possibility that the bias error found in a particular system of measurement will be present throughout the equipment's entire operating range. It is important to know whether a measurement system can be trusted for large as well as small values. Linearity analysis often is used during the measure stage of DMAIC. In this stage, linearity analysis is useful for assessing the accuracy of a measurement system within the range of values likely to be observed during the process. The standard procedure for analyzing linearity was established by the Automotive Industry Action Group. The first step selecting multiple parts to examine throughout the operating range.

A reference value should be obtained with precise equipment. The next step is having different employees measure the parts throughout the range with the intended measurement system. The average of these measurements should be found, and then the bias can be calculated by subtracting the average measurement from the reference value. This data then should be depicted on a scatter diagram. The adequacy of the measurement system is assessed using R^2, the coefficient of determination. A value of greater than 70% is acceptable in most cases.

Metrology

Metrology is the study of measurement. It is concerned with the quality of measurement systems, the appropriateness of various metrics, and the systems for creating new forms of measurement. One aspect of metrology is the development of protocols for assessing measurement systems. Six Sigma projects focus primarily on scientific and applied metrology. Scientific metrology is the development of quantity systems, unit systems, and new methods of measurement. Scientific metrology is a theoretical branch of metrology, although efforts are made to devise means of transferring traceability, or the degree to which a measurement can be compared with known standards. Applied metrology, on the other hand, is the use of measurement systems in manufacturing and other processes. This branch of metrology is more practical, focusing on the tools and methods that normal people can use to achieve accurate, traceable, and repeatable measurements.

Metrological traceability
Metrological traceability is the degree to which a measurement can be compared confidently to a known standard. Most people assume that the measurements they take are accurate: for instance, when

a person uses a ruler he or she never wonders whether the markings for inches are spaced correctly. However, in metrology, generally every measurement is assumed as somewhat inaccurate. As a result, knowing exactly how inaccurate a measurement is likely to be, on average, is important. A measurement system is considered more traceable when the uncertainties can be calculated and accounted. A measurement is considered traceable when it can be compared effectively with measurements taken at different times and in different conditions. In Six Sigma applications, where the degree of precision is extremely important, it also will be crucial for each successive measurement in a designed experiment to have the same level of traceability.

Those persons concerned with measurement systems are always trying to improve the traceability of their metrics. In most cases, this means coming up with better systems for calibrating measurement devices. Calibration is the process of checking to see that a measurement device has a close relationship with a known standard. Various international organizations maintain standard weights and measures. Among these organizations are the National Institute of Standards and Technology and the National Physical Laboratory in England. In more complex traceability operations, two distinct metrics are compared until they can be calibrated against one another. In other words, researchers will determine the range of traceability for one metric then the range of traceability for another, and then they will examine the relationship between the two metrics in the areas where these ranges overlap.

Measurement uncertainty

Applied metrology is essentially the struggle to reduce measurement uncertainty, also known as error. The extent to which a measurement is incorrect must be susceptible to measurement. Metrology assumes that almost every measurement contains some degree of error, but in order for a measurement system to be useful this degree of error must be regular. In a few cases, measurement error can be avoided, as such as when a detecting device registers a zero. Metrology studies have been able to isolate situations in which common measurement errors are likely. One common tool for assessing measurement uncertainty is the analysis of variance (ANOVA) gauge repeatability and reproducibility study. The repeatability of a measurement is the degree to which measurements taken of the same object in the same conditions will be equal. Reproducibility is the degree to which measurements taken in different locations by different people will be equal.

Engineering tolerance and calibration

Calibration is the process of confirming that a measuring device produces values similar to known standards. The basic calibration process begins when the instrument of measurement is designed. The instrument should be durable enough to produce similar values repeatedly. The extent to which the instrument will maintain its powers over a long time is known as tolerance. The tolerance in most cases is established by the manufacturer and is listed on the instrument along with a range of acceptable conditions for use. The manufacturer also will indicate how long the instrument can be expected to maintain its quality if used at a standard rate. For instance, if the product is to be used twelve hours a day, five days a week, it might be expected to last three months. After this interval, it cannot be relied upon to produce accurate measurements.

Basic calibration process

The basic calibration process requires the definition of measurement uncertainty for both the standard and the measuring instrument. The general rule is that the standard should have at the most a quarter of the measurement uncertainty, or error, as the instrument. If this is the case, any discrepancies caused by variation in the standard should have a negligible effect on the final results of the calibration process. As measuring devices have become more precise, however, it has become more difficult for standards to maintain this advantage. When the measuring device is as accurate or nearly as accurate as the standard, however, it is possible to adjust the accuracy of the measuring device in order to achieve the desired ratio. Another solution to this problem is to adjust the calibration tolerance for the instrument.

Central limit theorem

In some cases, there will not be enough (or good enough) data to establish a distribution. The central limit theorem is applied when the true distribution of a population is unknown. The central limit theorem, in short, asserts that the probability distribution of the sample means will approach a normal distribution as the number of samples increases, provided that they are simple random samples of uniform size. The central limit theorem is applied in cases when the number of samples is relatively small or when the true distribution is unknown. After about thirty samples, the data should approximate a normal distribution. The central limit theorem is extremely useful in control charting and in the calculation of process capability.

Box-whisker charts

Box-whisker charts are graphs used for the comparison of summary data from numerous data sets. The data sets may be organized by any general principle or characteristic. Box-whisker charts may be used in the analyze and improve stages of DMAIC. During the analyze stage, box-whisker charts may be used to compare the placement and characteristics of services, products, or processes. During the improve stage, box-whisker charts may be used to compare process performance before and after improvement efforts. It should be noted that box-whisker charts do not contain statistical control limits and therefore cannot be used to baseline or set statistical controls for a process. In other words, box-whisker charts are not control charts.

Creation
A box-whisker chart features horizontal and vertical axes. Above each mark on the horizontal axis, a bisected box with lines, or whiskers, will extend from the top and bottom. The upper and lower edges of the box indicate the dimensions of the first and third quartiles of data. The whiskers indicate the upper and lower limits according to special formulae. The lower limit is calculated with the formula Lower Limit = Q1 – 1.5 × (Q3 – Q1). The upper limit is calculated with the formula Upper Limit = Q3 + 1.5 × (Q3 – Q1). Typically, the box and whiskers should be based on quartiles; however, with normal distributions it is also possible to use metrics like mean and standard deviations. For instance, the box could define ± 2 standard deviations, and the whiskers could indicate ± 4 standard deviations. Some box-whisker charts will include dots beyond the upper and lower limits, indicating the greatest and least data points, respectively. Before creating and interpreting a box-whisker chart, establishing appropriate statistical controls is essential.

Scatter diagrams

A scatter diagram is a simple plot on two axes, useful for investigating the correlation between two variables. Scatter diagrams are used during the analyze stage of DMAIC. The x-axis of a scatter diagram measures the independent variable (is the variable manipulated in the experiment) and the y-axis measures the dependent variable (the variable not manipulated in the experiment). The general method of an experiment involves making small adjustments to the independent variable and observing the effects on the dependent variable. The independent variable should be manipulated throughout the entire region of interest, so data points achieve sufficient spread on the diagram. Also, the data used on a scatter diagram should be generated especially for that purpose. Experimenters should be cautious when one variable appears to change along with another, since correlation does not imply causation. Perceived correlations suggest a need for further experimentation.

Histograms

A histogram is a tool for presenting data pictorially. It looks like a standard bar graph, except that each bar represents the total number of observations that lie within a range of ranked values. Histograms may be used during the measure and analyze stages of DMAIC. In these stages, histograms are useful for identifying multiple distributions for applying a distribution to capability analysis. Histograms are created by first placing all data in order from least to greatest. The number of bars in a histogram should equal the square root of the total set of data values. The width of each bar is the quotient of the range of data and the number of bars. The range of the data is calculated by subtracting the minimum value from the maximum value.

Next, one should determine the number of data observations in each bar. The horizontal axis of the histogram will indicate the data values for each bar, and the vertical axis will indicate the number of observations.

Interpretation
Histograms effectively pinpoint the process location and variation. Histograms also indicate when data is symmetrical or bounded. A symmetrical distribution is characterized by data spread evenly about the histogram's center in an arrangement similar to a bell curve. If the histogram is more skewed, the data is not distributed evenly. For instance, if the data has more than one peak, it may have been obtained from multiple sources. A histogram only indicates the performance of the process as it is being measured. If the sample period was extended, the output would be considerably broader. Also, histograms do not take the sequence of the points into account, so they must be accompanied by measures of statistical process control. It is important to use a control chart to identify statistical control before fitting a distribution.

Process baseline estimation

Enumerative statistics
In process baseline estimation, enumerative statistics are useful for evaluating random samples from populations. For instance, these techniques can be used to determine whether two samples were drawn from a known population, as well as whether the samples were drawn from the same population. Enumerative statistics can determine whether samples represent the population, meaning that they were drawn without bias. Enumerative statistics can provide a confidence level, an assumed distribution, and a set of confidence intervals as well. In most cases, the confidence level will be 95%.

Confidence intervals are the upper and lower boundaries for the value of the statistic given the data. The only problem with enumerative statistical methods is that they are drawn from a static, unchanging population. In Six Sigma, often it is necessary to obtain information about dynamic processes. For this, analytical statistics are required.

Analytical statistics

Analytical statistics can provide information about processes in action. These techniques distinguish common- and special-cause variation. Common-cause variation occurs consistently and always influences data in a similar fashion. Special-cause variation, on the other hand, is unpredictable in its occurrence and effects. Statistical process control charts create an operational definition of special-cause variation by noting the location and level of variation within a subgroup at each time in the process. If enough subgroups can be collected, the statistical process control chart will be able to predict the location and extent of special-cause variation. The key feature of analytical statistics is the consideration of time, which makes it possible to pinpoint the moments in a process that need improvement.

Probability

Six Sigma professionals examine processes that are subject to occasional defects or variations. Predicting exactly when or how these events will occur is not always possible, even when measuring the rate of occurrence is possible. Many Six Sigma calculations, then, require probabilistic thinking. That is, Six Sigma professionals must be able to express the likelihood of a particular event. As an example, imagine a manufacturing process with a nonconformance rate of 1/50. In such a case, each customer would have a 2% chance of receiving a nonconforming product. One problem with generating probabilistic measurements like this is assuming that the sample represents the population as a whole. A special notation known as the complementation rule is used in probability. The probability of some event A occurring is written as $P(A)$, while the probability of A not occurring would be written $P(A')$. Therefore, the probability of A occurring is 1calculated $P(A) = 1 - P(A')$.

Multiple events

Six Sigma experts often have to consider the probabilities of several events at the same time. A special notation exists for these operations. The occurrence of A or B or both is called union and is written $A \cup B$. The occurrence of both A and B is called intersection and is written $A \cap B$. The occurrence of A but not B or B but not A is called difference and is written either $A - B$ or $B - A$. In the case of two events that cannot happen at the same time, the events are described as mutually exclusive or disjoint events. The probability of mutually exclusive events is written $P(A \cup B) = P(A) + P(B)$. The probability of two events that can occur at the same time is written $P(A \cup B) = P(A) + P(B) - P(A \cap B)$. As an example, consider a process in which task A has a 0.01 probability of failure and task B has a 0.02 rate of failure. The likelihood of a failure occurring during the process would be calculated $P(A \cup B) = P(A) + P(B) - P(A \cap B) = 0.01 + 0.02 - (0.01)(0.02) = 0.0302$.

General multiplication rule

In some situations, the occurrence of one event influences the probability of another event. For instance, when the occurrence of A changes the likelihood of B, the new probability for B is written $P(B|A)$. Now, the probability that both events will occur is calculated $P(A \cap B) = P(A) \times P(B|A)$. This is known as the general multiplication rule. One common example of the general multiplication rule is the probability of selecting a card from a certain suit out of a full deck. There are 52 cards in a deck and 13 in each suit, so the likelihood of drawing a spade is 13/52. If a spade is drawn the first time, the probability of drawing a spade again is 12/51, because there is one less card and one less spade in the deck. The probability of drawing two spades in a row can be calculated $P(A \cap B) = P(A) \times P(B|A) = (13/52)(12/51) = (0.25)(0.235) = 0.059$, or about 6%. In cases where the two events are independent, the chance that both will occur is calculated $P(A \cap B) = P(A) \times P(B)$.

Takt time

Takt time, which can be translated roughly from the German as "cycle time," is a reasonable assessment of the time required to complete each step in a manufacturing process. The combination of takt times is the overall length of the manufacturing process. In order for the product or service to be completed within the target interval, takt times for each step must be observed. Takt time can be calculated by dividing the total amount of time available to work by the number of units required per day. The amount of time available to work is expressed in minutes of work per unit produced, and the customer demand is expressed in required units per day, so takt time will be expressed as the minutes of work required to produce a unit. The calculation of takt time should include the inevitable delays and breaks.

Pros and cons

The implementation of a takt time system makes production evaluation much easier. Takt time requires products to move along a linear path, so any obstacles or hindrances to continuous production should be identifiable. Establishing a takt time for each task encourages employees to eliminate any activities not contributing directly to the accomplishment of goals. Also, the standardization of work processes means that employees will not be required to perform a wide variety of tasks, so they will be more consistent. Of course, employees will be performing the same tasks repeatedly, so a risk of boredom or burnout exists. Some businesses mitigate these risks by periodically rotating employees to different positions on the production path. One disadvantage of takt time systems is that increases in customer demand may require the creation of extra work stations, which can be difficult. Takt time systems also require that tasks be leveled, which eliminates bottlenecks but reduces flexibility.

Distributions

Statistical distributions allow Six Sigma teams to make performance assumptions with a minimum of supporting data. When discrete data is obtained, the binomial and Poisson distributions may be used. When the data is continuous, the normal, exponential, Johnson, and Pearson distributions are applicable. Discrete data is obtained from processes that can be counted. For instance, collections of error data usually will consist of the number of times the error occurred. Continuous data, on the other hand, is derived from measurement. As such, continuous data indicates not just the number of events, but also the extent of each event. Distributions may be useful in the measure, analyze, improve, and control stages of DMAIC. The primary utility of these tools involves determining the characteristics, most notably the sigma level, of processes and resources. Six Sigma professionals also may use these tools to create random data for use during process modeling.

Binomial and Poisson distributions

Binomial distributions are useful when the units in a population exist in only two states. For instance, if the only possible characteristics of a population are "off" and "on," a binomial distribution can be used to estimate the total number of "offs" and "ons" in a population. A binomial distribution only applies when trials are independent and the number of samples in the population is fixed. In a binomial distribution, the distributional parameter is the average proportion. This value is assumed or calculated by dividing the number of sample items that meet the condition by the total number of items in the sample. A Poisson distribution, on the other hand, can guess the number of times a particular condition will occur for a given process or population. The distinguishing feature of the Poisson distribution is its appropriateness for situations in which the targeted condition may occur more than once in each unit. The Poisson distribution accurately estimates the number of events in each sample unit. As with the binomial distribution, the trials be should be independent, and the data should be composed of positive whole numbers. In a Poisson distribution, the distributional parameter is the average number of instances per unit.

Exponential and lognormal distributions
Exponential distributions are used for continuous data, or data obtained by measurement. The most common application for this distribution is in the measurement of event rate, or the frequency with which a particular event occurs. If the event rate essentially is constant, the exponential distribution is appropriate. The distributional parameter is λ (lambda), calculated $1/\mu$, where μ is the interval between events. Lognormal distributions are appropriate for continuous data that has a fixed lower boundary, usually zero, and no upper boundary. This distribution is used often for reliability data. As with other distributions, a goodness-of-fit test can determine whether a lognormal

distribution credibly summarizes the data.

Normal distributions
Normal distributions are used for continuous data that have neither an upper nor a lower boundary. A normal distribution looks like the classic bell curve. For a normal distribution, the average of a sample, $\bar{X}$, is calculated by adding all the measurements and dividing by the total number of measurements, N. The standard deviation of N is calculated with the following formula:
$s = \dfrac{\sum_{j=1}^{N}(\bar{X}-X_1)^2}{N}$. One must the calculate a z value so this particular standard deviation may be considered a standardized normal distribution with a standard deviation of 1 and a mean of zero. The z value is calculated with $z = \dfrac{(X-\bar{X})}{s}$. Once this z value is obtained, it is possible to estimate the likelihood of being greater or less than a particular value for x.

Weibull and Johnson distributions
Weibull distributions are appropriate for continuous data with a set lower boundary, usually zero, and no upper boundary. Like the lognormal distribution, the Weibull distribution often applies to reliability data, in which the interval between failures is recorded. A Johnson distribution, on the other hand, is appropriate for continuous data on which neither a normal nor an exponential distribution may be used. Johnson distributions often are useful for data obtained after quality improvement campaigns, because the adjustments to process create non-results. A Johnson distribution assumes that the data represents the process during the period of collection and that one distribution accurately can represent the data. These assumptions are key because they assert that enough data has been collected to make visible any common causes of

variation. Johnson distributions are more provisional than others, although any statistical distribution should be taken with a grain of salt.

Parameters of statistical distribution

The four primary parameters of a statistical distribution are central tendency, skewness, standard deviation, and kurtosis. The central tendency is the general trend indicated by the data. In a symmetrical distribution such as the normal distribution, the mean is the best estimate of the central tendency. In an asymmetrical distribution, the median is a more accurate site of the central tendency. The skewness of a distribution is essentially the distance between the average and the mode, or the most-represented data value. A symmetrical distribution has no skew. Standard deviation indicates the average variation of data points from the mean. A measure of standard deviation suggests how close to the mean each data point likely will be. Finally, kurtosis is the sharpness of the distribution's peak. In a normal distribution, the kurtosis is 1. A distribution with a sharper peak will have a higher value for the kurtosis.

Process capability index

A process capability index quantifies the ability of a process to meet the expectations of customers and other stakeholders. This index usually is converted into a standard deviation or estimate of defects per million opportunities. Process capability indices typically are used during the measure, improve, and control stages of DMAIC. In the measure stage, process capability indices can create a baseline estimate for a controlled process. During the improve stage, a process capability index can confirm process improvements and assure the team that the process is in statistical control. In the control stage, these indices are used to monitor

processes, generally to confirm that they remain in a state of statistical control. For all of these uses, the process must be in statistical control. Otherwise, measures of process capability cannot be trusted. If the process has both upper and lower specifications, the statistics C_p and C_{pk} can be used. If only one of the specifications is known, C_{pk} must be used.

Creation

Before process capability can be calculated, it is necessary to use a control chart to determine the stability of the process. The capability indices for a normal distribution are calculated

$$C_p = \frac{\text{high spec} - \text{low spec}}{6\sigma_x}, \; C_{pk} = \min(Cp_l, Cp_u),$$

and $C_{pm} = \dfrac{C_p}{\sqrt{1 + \frac{(\bar{x}-T)^2}{\sigma_x^2}}}$. In these equations, $\bar{x}$

is the grand average, T is the process target, and σ_x is process sigma. If the subgroup size is 1, process sigma is calculated according to the moving-range statistic. If the subgroup size is greater than 1, the process sigma is calculated with the subgroup sigma statistic.

$$C_p = \frac{Z_L}{3} \qquad\qquad Cp_u = \frac{Z_u}{3}$$
$$Z_l = \frac{\bar{x} - \text{low spec}}{\sigma_x} \qquad Z_u = \frac{\text{high spec} - \bar{x}}{\sigma_x}$$

The capability indices for non-normal distributions are calculated with

$$C_p = \frac{\text{high spec} - \text{low spec}}{\text{ordinate}_{0.99865} - \text{ordinate}_{0.00135}},$$

$Z_l = |Z_{\text{normal},p}|$, and $Z_u = |Z_{\text{normal},1-p}|$. In these equations, $\text{ordinate}_{0.99865}$ and $\text{ordinate}_{0.00135}$ are the z values for the non-normal distribution curve at 99.865 and 0.135. Also, $Z_{\text{normal},p}$ and $Z_{\text{normal},1-p}$ are the z values of the normal cumulative distribution curve at the p and $1 - p$ percentage points, respectively.

Interpretation

A process capability index is influenced heavily by the distribution assumptions. If the value of C_p (the ratio of tolerance to process variation) is 1, then tolerance and process variation are equal. If the value of

C_p is less than one, then the allowable variation is less than the process variation, which means that the normal amount of variation could be too much. This is a bad situation. When C_{pk} is used, it is possible to obtain information about the process variation and location and their relation to the requirements. The statistic C_{pm} is much like C_{pk}, but it also considers the relation between process average and a target value. If these values are the same, then C_{pm} and C_{pk} are equal.

Process performance indices

A process performance index determines whether a particular batch of materials will be satisfactory to customers. That its scope is limited to a single batch distinguishes the process performance index from the process capability index. Process performance indices are used most often in the measure stage of DMAIC. In this stage, they are used to create process baseline estimates for uncontrolled processes. To do so, however, the sample must be quite largein order to assess any variations in the batch. In most cases, statistical process controls are preferred over process performance indices. However, sometimes statistical process controls will not be possible, whether because the process lacks statistical control or because there is insufficient data.

Creation
If the batch sample has both upper and lower specifications, then the P_p statistic may be used. When only one of the specifications is present, the P_{pk} statistic can be used. The performance indices for normal distributions are calculated

$$P_p = \frac{\text{high spec}-\text{low spec}}{6\sigma_x}, \; P_{pk} = \min(Pp_l, Pp_u),$$

and $p_{pm} = \dfrac{p_p}{\sqrt{1+\frac{(\bar{\bar{x}}-T)^2}{\sigma_x^2}}}$. In these equations, $\bar{\bar{x}}$

is the grand average, T is the process target, and σ_x is the sample sigma.

$$P_{pl} = \frac{Z_l}{3} \qquad P_{pu} = \frac{Z_u}{3} \qquad Z_l =$$
$$\frac{\bar{\bar{x}}-\text{low spec}}{\sigma_x} \qquad Z_u = \frac{\text{high spec}-\bar{\bar{x}}}{\sigma_x}$$

When the distributions are non-normal, performance indices are calculated as

$$C_p = \frac{\text{high spec}-\text{low spec}}{\text{ordinate}_{0.99865}-\text{ordinate}_{0.00135}},$$

$Z_l = |Z_{\text{normal},p}|$, and $Z_u = |Z_{\text{normal},1-p}|$. In these equations, $\text{ordinate}_{0.99865}$ and $\text{ordinate}_{0.00135}$ are the z values for the non-normal distribution curve at 99.865 and 0.135. Also, $Z_{\text{normal},p}$ and $Z_{\text{normal},1-p}$ are the z values of the normal cumulative distribution curve at the p and $1-p$ percentage points.

Interpretation
Unlike statistical control charts, process performance indices cannot be used to predict future performance. A measure of process performance incorporates sample sigma (that is, standard deviation), so it cannot suggest process capability for the future. Although using capability indices generally is better, when a process is in statistical control the calculation of process performance indices will be remarkably similar to process capability indices. If the process performance indices have values less than 1, then tolerance (variation that can be allowed) is less than the variation in the sample. If the value is 1, then the variation in the sample is exactly the same as the tolerance. The best result is to have process performance indice values of greater than 1, indicating that the sample variation is less than the allowable variation.

Identification of key decision points

Once the process map has been created, it can be used to identify the most important decisions made during the process. Team members will especially be alert to any areas that seem to require excessive decision-making, usually a sign of inefficiency. As much as possible, the team will want to reduce the number of decisions that have to be made every time a process is performed. All stakeholders must be aware that changes are not to be made to the process at this time. Since the process has not yet been measured, it is essential that all measurements reflect the process as typically performed. Otherwise, improvement efforts could be targeted incorrectly. The team leader needs to communicate this information to all stakeholders.

Basic objectives of the measure stage

During the measure stage of DMAIC, the Six Sigma team will focus on gathering the information necessary to complete the project. First, the team will attempt to define each relevant process in great detail. At the same time, it will be necessary to develop a group of metrics appropriate to the processes. No metric is complete until accompanied by a measurement analysis system that identifies and quantifies any common errors in the metric. In other words, the team will need to determine the ways in which the measurement system likely is inaccurate. The final general objective of the measure phase is to estimate process baselines. This objective enables the team to identify a reasonable starting point for the project.

Identification of process metrics

One of the key tasks of the measure stage is to identify process metrics. Typically, quite a few process metrics can provide useful information about a particular process. These metrics tend to relate to schedule, cost, or quality. Factors critical to schedule (CTS) have a direct bearing on the completion date of the process. Factors critical to quality (CTQ) have a direct effect on the desired characteristics of the product or service. Factors critical to cost (CTC) have an impact on materials, labor, delivery, overhead, inventory, and/or the cost to the consumer of the

good or service. As much as possible, these metrics should be customer-focused and transparent: that is, they should provide immediate objective data that can be analyzed. Moreover, these metrics need to be obtained with measurement systems that are repeatable and reproducible.

Process definition

The first major step in the measure stage is to create a comprehensive process level map of processes as currently performed. In other words, during this stage the group defines and clearly describes all of the activities they aim to improve. This is a much more detailed and comprehensive version of the top-level process map created in the define stage. A detailed process map typically requires the participation of expert employees. This participation is important especially because employees may have a vastly different conception of process sequence than their superiors. Often, employees will have streamlined or modified a process without notifying management. Judging the beneficiality of customizations made by employees is unnecessary and potentially harmful. The primary concern at this point is to create an accurate map of the process as currently performed.

Top-level process definition

The most common tool for top-level process definition is the flowchart. A flowchart does a good job of representing process sequences graphically, with a minimum of verbal description. The look of a flowchart is very easy to read. When the team wants to identify inputs, outputs, and stakeholders, SIPOC (suppliers, inputs, processes, outputs, customers) analysis is more appropriate. Another tool is the process map, which is similar to the flowchart, although it contains more detail. A process map indicates who is responsible for each activity in the process. A comprehensive Six Sigma project might include more than one of these tools for top-level process definition. The primary aim of these representations is to inform stakeholders and other people peripheral to the project. A top-level process definition will not contain enough information to explain each process in depth.

Process metrics

Process metrics must be reliable, repeatable, and reproducible. Otherwise, they cannot be considered effective illustrations of process characteristics. At the same time, measurements must be specific and detailed enough to distinguish between the effects of process alterations and process noise. As much as possible, metrics should relate to actual targets of business strategy and should result from cooperation between employees. Before any metrics are applied, employees from several different departments should judge them. If possible, metrics should be related to actual services provided to customers. Finally, metrics should pertain to values critical to quality, schedule, or cost, as these factors are the three most important variables in any process.

Analyze Stage

Primary objectives of the analyze stage

In the analyze stage of DMAIC, the Six Sigma team will focus on analyzing the sources of variation in the target process. This analysis may require the use of sophisticated statistical tools. The team also will analyze the value stream. The value stream is the set of activities that create value for the customer. During the analyze stage, the team will identify the process drivers, which are the activities that exert a significant influence on the results of processes. Obviously, the intention of the Six Sigma efforts will be to enhance those activities that add value and to eliminate those activities that take up time and resources without adding much value. The value stream only includes those activities necessary for the creation of the product or service. The judgment of value should be from the perspective of the customer rather than from the perspective of stakeholders within the company.

Confidence interval on mean

One of the more useful forms of statistical inference is the estimation of confidence interval on mean, which requires a population sample. This technique can be useful during the measure and analyze stages of DMAIC. The use of this technique assumes that the sample represents the entire population and that it has a normal distribution. Also, the sample should be constant, meaning that it can be assumed to remain relatively stable through time. During the measure stage, an estimation of confidence interval on mean is used to estimate the process average when a process control cannot be set because of a lack of data. This process average is used for baseline estimates. In the analyze stage, an estimation of the confidence interval on mean is used to examine the similarities and differences between the sample means taken during various process conditions.

Process when the historical standard deviation is known

When the historical standard deviation is known, the process of estimating the confidence interval on the mean begins with calculating the average $\bar{X}$ for n sample units. The confidence interval may then be calculated with the following formula: $\bar{X} - Z_{\alpha/2}(\sigma/\sqrt{n}) < \mu < \bar{X} + Z_{\alpha/2}(\sigma/\sqrt{n})$. In this approach, it is assumed that the samples are taken from a population with a normal distribution. Therefore, the z values are calculated according to the confidence level. If the confidence level is 90%, then $\alpha = 0.1$. The confidence interval is two-sided: that is, it extends from one side of the mean to the other. Therefore, the α value is divided in two: $\alpha/2 = 0.05$. The z value, then, can be obtained by referring to a chart of areas under the normal curve.

Process when the historical standard deviation is unknown

In some cases, the historical standard deviation is unknown, and so an alternate method for estimating the confidence interval on the mean must be used. First, one must calculate the average $\bar{X}$ and the sample standard deviation s for n sample units. The confidence interval is calculated with the formula $\bar{X} - t_{\alpha/2,n-1}(s/\sqrt{n}) < \mu < \bar{X} + t_{\alpha/2,n-1}(s/\sqrt{n})$. As with a known historical standard deviation, it is assumed that the samples are taken from a population with a normal distribution. Again, the confidence interval will be two-sided, so confidence level should be divided by two. Confidence interval calculations can be executed in both Minitab and Excel, although in Minitab one must have the raw data in order to proceed.

Interpretation

An estimation of the confidence interval on the mean indicates the percentage of samples that will contain the true population mean, otherwise known as μ (mu). For example, if the confidence limit on the mean is estimated at 97%, one can expect that 97% of samples the confidence interval will include μ. The estimation of the true mean becomes more assured as the number of sampled increases. In other words, the confidence interval and the number of samples are inversely proportionate. This estimation is more powerful when the standard deviation, or σ, is known. When the standard deviation is unknown, the *t* tables must be used. When the standard deviation is known, the *z* tables may be used.

Confidence interval on proportion

In some cases, analysts will have a solid history of the standard deviation for a given population. In such cases, analysts can estimate the confidence level of the mean at a particular confidence level. This statistical technique can be useful during the measure and analyze stages of DMAIC. As with the confidence interval on mean, the sample being used must represent the entire population, must be constant, and must have a normal distribution. In the measure stage, this technique is useful in situations where limited data exists for the purposes of establishing a process control. In such a case, estimations of the confidence interval on proportion can be used to estimate the average error rates for processes.

Process

To estimate the confidence interval on proportion, begin by calculating the average error rate $\hat{p}$ for *n* sample units. The confidence interval is then calculated with the formula

$$\hat{p} - Z_{\alpha/2}\sqrt{\frac{\hat{p}(1-\hat{p})}{n}} \le p \le \hat{p} + Z_{\alpha/2}\sqrt{\frac{\hat{p}(1-\hat{p})}{n}}.$$

As with estimate of the confidence interval on proportion, this operation assumes that the samples are taken from a population with a normal distribution. Also, the confidence interval is two-sided, running from one side of the mean to the other. The *z* value can be obtained from a table that outlines areas under the standard normal curve.

Interpretation

The confidence interval on proportion indicates the percentage of samples in which the confidence interval will include the true error rate. For example, if the confidence limit on the error rate is calculated as 90%, it may be assumed that nine out of ten samples will include the true error rate if the confidence interval is reached. As with the interval on the mean, the confidence interval on proportion decreases as the number of samples increases. In other words, when more samples are obtained, fewer values are required to create confidence. The opposite is true, as well: when the number of samples is small, a larger confidence interval is required. Process stability cannot be determined simply by the fact that a particular sample falls within the confidence interval. Process stability must be confirmed with a statistical process control chart.

Regression analysis

Regression analysis is a system for identifying when independent variables are influenced by one or more dependent variables. Regression analysis may be used during the measure, analyze, and improve stages of DMAIC. In the measure stage, regression analysis is used to evaluate the degree to which a measurement system is linear. During the analyze stage, regression analysis can be used to explore the connections between metrics and process factors. In the improve stage, regression analysis is useful for confirming these connections after improvements have been implemented. A scatter diagram often is interpreted with a simple linear regression analysis. If more than one factor influences the value of the independent variable, then multiple regression is necessary.

Simple linear regression
A simple linear regression tries to orient data points around a single straight line. In mathematics, the equation for this line is written $y = mx + b$, where y is the dependent variable, m is the slope, x is the independent variable, and b is the point along the y-axis where $x = 0$ (often referred to as the y-intercept). This is known as slope-intercept form. In Six Sigma, however, it is more common to see the formula expressed $Y = \beta_0 + \beta_1 X +$ error, where β_0 is the estimation of the intercept and β_1 is the regression line's slope. The values for intercept and slope typically are estimated according to the method of least squares, in which the line is drawn with a minimal squared distance to each data point. The statistical equation for a simple linear regression includes the word *error* as an acknowledgement that every set of data points will have some inaccuracies.

First-order model of multiple regression
If more than one factor influences a dependent variable, a multiple regression must be used. A multiple regression takes into account the interactions between these multiple factors. In a first-order model, the value of the dependent variable is based on the influence of each factor by itself, as well as each possible combination of two factors. Whatever error exists in the model is assumed to be the same for all factors and combinations of factors. A first-order multiple regression usually will produce an essentially straight line over small regions, so it can be useful when only targeted data is needed. Examined from a more distant perspective, however, the model will appear as a linear regression for which the plane has been curved or twisted. This flexing of the plane is caused by the influence of interacting factors.

Higher-order models of multiple regression
When more complex analysis is required for a process in which more than one factor influences a dependent variable, a higher-order model of multiple regression must be performed. For instance, a higher-order multiple regression can include squares and cubes of the values, which will produce a response surface with definable peaks and valleys. A higher-order multiple regression is valuable only if exhaustive experiments already have been performed on the main effects. Multiple regression models with higher orders are useful for mapping smaller regions, in particular peaks, valleys, and minimaxes (intersections between the minimum for one factor and the maximum for another). Higher-order multiple regression models also are good at defining the area that surrounds a stationary point. In Six Sigma, these models often are used to evaluate how current operating parameters influence the response.

Residuals analysis

Residuals are the differences between a response's observed value and a regression model's predicted value for that response. A residuals analysis of a regression model will reveal any unusual patterns that could suggest error in the model. In statistical terms, this is expressed $e_i = y_i - \hat{y}_i$. Statistical software programs such as Excel will calculate a standardized residual $e_i/\sqrt{s^2}$, such that the variance is set to 1. This makes outliers more obvious. Perhaps the most common technique of residuals analysis is the normality test, in which the randomness of error is tested by creating a distribution of the residuals. If the error truly is random, then the residuals should follow a normal distribution with a mean of zero. Residuals also can be used on a scatter diagram to assess the independence of a variable.

Multi-vari plots

Multi-vari plots are effective tools for assessing the variation within samples or within particular parts. Multi-vari plots also can be used to analyze variation over time or between different batches. Multi-vari plots are used during the analyze stage of DMAIC. In this stage, they are primarily used to isolate the causes of variation and to obtain more information about the interactions among factors. The first step in constructing a multi-vari plot is determining the system for gathering data. This data should then be placed on a plot, with each sample unit represented by a different symbol. The length of each symbol will indicate the variation within the sample. The point of a multi-vari plot is to isolate the causes of variation. However, this tool is not a control chart, so it will not indicate whether the process is unstable from a statistical perspective.

Equality-of-variance tests

Equality-of-variance tests determine whether a similar degree of variation exists in particular subsets of data. This question is important because an effective analysis of variance cannot be performed unless equal variance has been established. Equality-of-variance tests are used primarily during the analyze and improve stages. During these stages, the tests are useful for assessing the observed data obtained during an analysis of variance. Equality-of-variance tests also may be used after regression analysis in order to assess the residuals. A few

different forms of this test exist. The most typical statistical test used to measure equality of variance is the Bartlett, although versions also are offered on Levene and Minitab. The Levene test is recommended in situations where non-normality is a strong possibility.

The most common test for equality of variance is the Bartlett, the appropriate test when the regression residuals are expected to follow a normal distribution. In the Bartlett test, the equality of the treatment variances is compared with the possibility that one variance is unequal to the others. The null hypothesis of the test holds that the subsets have equal variances, which is expressed as $H_o: \sigma^2_1 = \sigma^2_1 = \sigma^2_2 = \cdots = \sigma^2_a$, where a is the set of experimental conditions. If the null hypothesis is false, then at least one of the subsets must have an unequal variance. In order to assess the variance at each position, one must have more than one sample from each test condition. When non-normal variance is apparent, the variable in question can be transformed, which will mitigate its effect.

Control charts to identify sources of variation

In the analyze stage of DMAIC, the Six Sigma team will look closely at the statistical control charts created during the measure stage. One of the initial goals of analysis will be to distinguish special and common causes of variation. Special causes of variation do not occur during every performance of the process, but when they do, they cause significant delay. On a control chart, special causes of variation will be indicated by points that lie far outside the normal range. The location of these out-of-control points will suggest possible sources of the variation. That is, it will be possible to see at which point during the process the variation occurred. Common causes of variation will influence each iteration of the process and therefore will not be obvious on a control chart. Several reasons for common cause variation may exist. Variations from common cause, then, may be more difficult to diagnose.

U charts

U charts are control charts designed to handle attributes data. A U chart depicts the percentage of samples that have a particular condition in situations where sample sizes may vary and each sample may have more than one occurrence of the condition. U charts are used during the measure and improve stages of DMAIC. In the measure stage, they use attributes data to estimate process baselines. In most cases, however, it is better to use a variable control chart for this purpose. In the improve stage, U charts occasionally are used to establish target figures, though the relative paucity of errors makes it difficult to use these chart so late in the project. In a U chart, the plotted statistic is $u_j = \frac{(\text{count})_j}{n_j}$, where n_j is the sample size of group j. The centerline is $\bar{u} = \frac{\sum_{j=1}^{m}(\text{count})_j}{m}$, where m is the number of groups in the analysis. The upper control limits are $\text{UCL} = \bar{u} + 3\sqrt{\frac{\bar{u}}{n_j}}$ and the lower control limits are $\text{LCL} = \max\left(0, \bar{u} - 3\sqrt{\frac{\bar{u}}{n_j}}\right)$, where $\bar{u}$ is the average percent.

Interpretation
On a U chart, the upper and lower control limits indicate the boundaries of expected process behavior. The variation of points that lie within the control limits is attributed to common causes, while any points outside the statistical control must be attributed to special causes. If no special-cause variation exists, then the process is stable enough to be predictable. When special causes of variation exist, they must be identified and eliminated. The Six Sigma team will need to brainstorm possible sources of special-cause variation and then design experiments to test these hypotheses. In the meantime, it is possible to predict the behavior of the process once the special causes of variation have been removed. To make such a prediction, simply ignore all out-of-control points when calculating the average and the upper and lower control limits.

Hypothesis testing

Hypothesis testing establishes a degree of confidence and then compares a sample statistic against a historical value or another sample statistic. In other words, hypothesis testing allows one to make statistical inferences about the characteristics of a population. This sort of testing is useful for distinguishing the factors that contribute to variation in data. Primarily, this type of testing is used during designed experiments and regression analysis. Hypothesis testing often is performed during the analyze and improve stages of DMAIC. In the improve stage, its primary function is comparing the averages of improved processes with baseline estimates. In order to perform hypothesis testing, the population must be assumed constant and homogenous. Also, that samples are random and representative must be assumed.

Process
The first step in hypothesis testing is stating the null hypothesis, H_0. In most cases, the null hypothesis represents the value that the test aspires to prove. Since a hypothesis test only can reject the null hypothesis or fail to reject it, in some cases framing the null hypothesis as something to be disproved makes more sense. The next step in hypothesis testing is defining the alternative hypothesis (H_1). The alternative hypothesis should cover all of the area excluded from the null

hypothesis. The third step is either setting a value for p or selecting a significance level (α). The significance level is the chance of incorrectly rejecting a true hypothesis in what is known as a Type 1 error. Generally, it is considered better to set a p value because this allows more freedom for adjustment later in the experiment. Next, samples are collected and statistics are calculated. The final step in hypothesis testing is drawing a conclusion.

Interpretation

Interpreting a hypothesis test is simple. If the calculated statistic is larger than the critical value of the test statistic for the given level of significance, then the null hypothesis must be rejected. If the critical value of the test statistic is larger, then the null hypothesis is not rejected. Software programs such as Excel or Minitab can use the calculated p value to indicate whether the obtained results are appropriate, assuming that the null hypothesis is true. If the p value is small, then the chances of obtaining results similar to those gathered during the experiment are so small that the null hypothesis should be rejected. If the null hypothesis is not rejected, the experiment is said to have reached a weak conclusion, because the means may or may not be equal. When the null hypothesis is confirmed, however, the experiment is said to have produced a strong conclusion, or a definitive statement that the means are not equal.

ANOVA

An analysis of variance (ANOVA) is a table that depicts the sum-of-squares variance that can be credited to a particular source, the sum of the squares that can be credited to error, and the total sum of squares from the data. This table includes F statistics related to the significance of the source relative to the error. An analysis of variance may be performed

during the measure or analyze stages of DMAIC. During the measure stage, analysis of variance is used to identify the origins of errors in measurement. This analysis is useful especially for processes that damage or diminish the resources involved, such that a repeatability and reproducibility (R & R) is not possible. In the analyze stage, analysis of variance can be used to gather information about the statistical significance of a regression models. Six Sigma teams often will use ANOVA in this manner to pinpoint possible process drivers. Another use of analysis of variance in the analyze stage is to identify differences between data subsets with the intention of identifying the causes of variation within a process.

In an analysis of variance, variation within each subgroup is compared to the variation found between different subgroups. The variation within each subgroup is found by sampling from the subgroup repeatedly. The variation between different subgroups is found by analyzing the essential differences between the averages of each subgroup. Analysis of variance begins with the null hypothesis, that all subgroup averages are equal. Then, the F statistic is used to compare the average variation between subsets, known as the mean square treatment, with the sun of the squares of the residuals, known as the mean square error. An F test assumes that subsets have a normal distribution and equal variance. If the p value for the F test is less than 0.05, then the null hypothesis can be rejected. This suggests that one or more of the subset averages is different.

Goodness-of-fit tests

A number of useful goodness-of-fit tests measure the validity of statistical assessment. In other words, these tests indicate whether a chosen statistical test provide an accurate and relevant measure. Goodness-of-fit tests may be

- 60 -

used during the measure, analyze, improve, and control stages of DMAIC. During these stages, the tests are used to confirm a distribution. This confirmation enables the team to assume the validity of confidence tests, statistical control charts, hypothesis tests, and other tests. Some of the most common goodness-of fit tests are the chi-square, Anderson-Darling, and Kolmogorov-Smirnov (K-S). The simplest of these tests is the chi-square, which can be explained and run without the need for special software. The Anderson-Darling and Kolmogorov-Smirnov tests are more specific, however, and provide better results when used appropriately.

Creation and interpretation

Most experts agree that a distributional fit cannot be tested properly without at least two hundred data points. However, if a process is not in statistical control, no distribution will fit its data points. In the Kolmogorov-Smirnov test, the actual data points generally will vary slightly from the curve that best charts their values. This difference should decrease as the number of data points rises. The K-S test essentially checks to see if this inverse relationship exists. The Anderson-Darling test, on the other hand, emphasizes the data obtained at the extreme ends of the distribution. In the assessment of a normal distribution, the mean should be approximately the value of the line as it passes through the 50th percentile. If too much data falls in the tails of the distribution, then there will be an abundance of points above the confidence interval on the left side and below the confidence interval on the right. Goodness-of-fit tests have a null hypothesis that the data follows the distribution in question. The measure of this fit is known as the p value. Typically, a larger p value indicates better fit.

Kruskal-Wallis and Mood's median tests

The Kruskal-Wallis and Mood's median tests are nonparametric estimation methods. The Kruskal-Wallis test is similar to the Mann-Whitney, and it is used in place of a one-way analysis of variance. In a Kruskal-Wallis test, the null hypothesis asserts that all medians are equal, and the alternative hypothesis asserts that the medians are not all equal. The Mood's median test, meanwhile, is a chi-square test. Again, the null hypothesis asserts that all the population medians are equal, and the alternative hypothesis asserts that the population medians are not all equal. The Kruskal-Wallis and Mood's median tests assume that the independent random samples drawn from different populations have a continuous distribution with the same shape. In general, the Mood's median test better handles outliers, while the Kruskal-Wallis is more powerful when dealing with some distributions.

Nonparametric tests on equality of means

Nonparametric tests occasionally are used in place of traditional hypothesis tests for the equality of two means. These tests are more effective when the assumptions associated with common statistical distributions cannot be met. Nonparametric tests are used during the analyze and improve stages of DMAIC. In the analyze stage, nonparametric tests are used to compare the means from samples with different conditions. In the improve stage, they are used to assess whether process averages have been improved over baseline estimates after the implementation of changes. These tests do not require statistical normality or any other quality in order to be valid. One disadvantage of this form of testing is its requirement of a larger sample size.

Nonparametric tests are available in every version of statistical software.

Creation and interpretation

For a nonparametric test on the equality of means, the null hypothesis H_0 will be that population 1's median is equal to population 2's median. The alternative hypothesis H_1, then, is that population 1's median does not equal population 2's median. Median is preferable to mean in these tests because it indicates central tendency regardless of distribution. The next step in the test involves declaring a significance level or p value. After samples have been collected, the probability of Type II error can be assessed. Upon completing the test, it is possible to compare the calculated statistics with a test statistic. The null hypothesis is rejected if the calculated statistic is greater than the critical value of the test statistic. If the calculated statistic does not exceed the critical value of the test statistic, then the null hypothesis cannot be rejected. Nonetheless, this rejection does not imply confirmation of the null hypothesis.

FMEA

Failure modes and effects analysis (FMEA) is a system for identifying extremely risky processes or features. The main criterion for this identification is that either the failure of the process will be very damaging or that a failure could occur unnoticed. Failure modes and effects analysis is primarily useful during the analyze, improve, and design stages of DMAIC. In the analyze stage, failure modes and effects analysis is used to identify and rank risky processes or product features. In the improve and design stages, failure modes and effects analysis is used to identify potentially risky activities or features in a planned improvement. A failure modes and effects analysis produces a risk priority number, which quantifies the severity, likelihood, and possibility for remediation of various accidents.

Creation

The creation of a failure modes and effects analysis (FMEA) begins with the identification of each step in a process or each feature in a product design. The next move is to identify all of the possible errors and mistakes for each step or feature. This list should be comprehensive, so it may take some time to create. The list also should indicate the results of each possible failure or error. In the next phase of FMEA, the severity of each possible failure or error should be ratedA number of standardized tables exist for ranking failure/error severity. Of course, it is impossible to rate the severity of failures in an objective manner. The next phase of FMEA is to gauge the likelihood of the failure or error. Again, this assessment typically is placed on a scale from one to ten. Next, the FMEA will focus on detection. The team should make a list of the mode of detection as well as the likelihood that failure will be detected (again, placed on a scale from one to ten). Finally, the ratings of severity, likelihood, and detection level are multiplied to produce a risk priority number (RPN). Possible failures are then ranked in order of descending RPN.

Interpretation

If severity, likelihood, and detection level each are rated on a ten-point scale, then the highest possible risk priority number will be 1000. The larger the number, the greater the risk. The interpretation and use of failure modes and effects analysis varies by organization. Some businesses establish a particular benchmark RPN and investigate any failures that score above it. One benefit of FMEA is its indication whether the severity, likelihood, or detection level of a failure needs attention. When severity must be reduced, redesigning the product or process entirely typically is necessary.

Reducing the likelihood of the failure often is the most cost-effective solution and therefore is a primary target of Six Sigma efforts. Reducing the detection level can be effective, but it does not improve the product or process in any way.

DFMEA and PFMEA

Failure modes and effects analysis (FMEA) is a tool for identifying and mitigating the sources of error in a process. Furthermore, two forms of FMEA exist: one for design (DFMEA) and one for processes (PFMEA). DFMEA is concerned with finding design defects that could result in malfunctions, a shorter product life, or hazards to the consumer. Most design-based businesses implement DFMEA tools throughout the creation of new products. PFMEA, on the other hand, is a tool for identifying and learning about potential errors in a service or production process. Specifically, PFMEA identifies failures that diminish the quality, reliability, or safety of a product or process. From the customer's perspective, identifying failures that will prevent alignment with desired specifications is important. Six Sigma businesses use PFMEA to achieve continuous improvement in processes.

Dashboards

A Six Sigma organization must have a group of metrics that reflect the current performance level and the possibility of upcoming problems. This set of metrics often is described as the dashboard because it serves the same purpose as the display panel in a car. A Six Sigma dashboard alerts employees that performance is sub-par or that problems are developing which could lead to a failure to meet objectives. To be effective, a dashboard should contain variables with a time component so changes can be assessed within the historical context. In addition, the factors displayed on the dashboard should be subjected to a statistical control chart. The Six Sigma dashboard should be available to all members of the organization.

Work breakdown structures

A work breakdown structure is a diagram that depicts the parts of a problem or process. These diagrams are useful when a problem seems overwhelming, because they break the problem down into manageable "sub-problems." Work breakdown structures are most useful during the define and analyze stages of DMAIC. In the define stage, work breakdown structures are combined with Pareto analysis to organize problems before solutions are applied. A work breakdown structure also may be useful at this time to eliminate less important areas of a project and thereby ensure adherence to a schedule. In the analyze stage, work breakdown structures are used to organize all of the issues and complaints to be handled during the improve stage. The completion of a work breakdown structure often suggests that different solutions should be applied to different parts of a general problem.

Creation and interpretation

A work breakdown structure is created first by breaking a problem into components. Each component of the problem subsequently should be broken down into categories. These categories should represent the different ways the particular problem can occur. The intention of the work breakdown structure is to reduce complex problems to a collection of discrete and manageable issues. The organization of a complex situation creates a map for problem solving that can be used by members of different departments. A comprehensive and effective work breakdown structure will create material for other data-organization charts such as Pareto charts.

The information displayed on a work breakdown structure would be prioritized on the resulting Pareto chart.

"5 Whys" method of problem-solving

The "5 Whys" method is used to identify the underlying causes of a defect. The method is simple: the problem is stated, and the questioner asks why this problem exists. For example, if the problem is that workers always are late, the questioner will ask, "Why are the workers always late?" An answer is given, and this statement is then questioned. This pattern continues until the root cause is identified. A continuation of the above example might proceed as follows: "The workers always are late because parking takes a long time." "Why?" "Because there aren't enough parking spaces." "Why?" "Because the company trucks are taking up multiple spaces in the lot...." And so on, until the root problem is identified and solved. More or less than five "whys" may be required to resolve the problem. This number was chosen as a guideline rather than a rule.

Criticisms
Some people criticize the "5 Whys" method of identifying underlying problems for being simplistic. One complaint about this method asserts that it encourages investigators to examine and resolve only the symptoms of a problem rather than addressing the true cause. Also, the "5 Whys" method does not require any further data-gathering, so it tends to be limited by the investigator's existing expertise. Furthermore, no part of the method encourages the investigator to consider a perspective other than his or her own. In addition, the "5 Whys" method tends to generate non-repeatable results, which cannot be duplicated or achieved by other investigators. One last criticism of the "5 Whys" method concerns its focus upon a single root cause while ignoring the possibility that a problem may have more than one cause.

Pareto charts

A Pareto chart is a form of bar graph in which problems are ranked according to their urgency. Each of the categories represented along the horizontal axis of a Pareto chart are exclusive, meaning that no single issue can fit into multiple categories. This characteristic is important because the category distinctions on a Pareto chart are largely subjective. Pareto charts are used during the define and analyze stages of DMAIC to guide the dispersal of resources and time to the most important issues. The categories on a Pareto chart are organized in descending order from left to right, according to whatever metric is deemed most appropriate. Most experts recommend that the metric be related either to count or to cost. Percentages and rates are not valid metrics for a Pareto chart.

Creating a Pareto chart
The first step in creating a Pareto chart involves identifying the correct categories. These categories should be non-overlapping and fungible. The count/cost metric will be along the left axis of the chart, and the identities of the categories will be along the bottom axis. Data should be collected over the same interval for each category. The categories will be placed in descending order from left to right. An indication of the percent demarcations, or the percent of total cost/count represented by each variable, will run along the right vertical axis. The cumulative percentages from each bar are indicated with a line ascending from left to right. This cumulative aspect of the Pareto chart makes percentages and rates unacceptable as data. In order for the chart to work, the data must be additive.

Interpretation

Pareto charts attempt to isolate the categories that contribute the most to count or cost. In addition, the cumulative line aspect of the chart indicates the degree to which resolving problems with the most pressing issues would improve performance. The traditional method for using a Pareto chart involves identifying the left-most categories that approximate 80% of the count or cost. These categories are the most important areas. A Pareto chart with a steep cumulative line is better because in such a chart, the value is concentrated in the left-most categories. A relatively flat cumulative bar is less helpful, because this arrangement indicates no problems as more important than the rest. When a Pareto chart is flat, the categories have been subdivided too much. In such instances, regrouping into a few large categories may bring about a better result.

Autocorrelation charts

Autocorrelation charts, otherwise known as the autocorrelation function (ACF), are used to determine the degree to which current data depends on previously gathered data. This is accomplished by automatically examining multiple observations of a particular characteristic with an eye toward possible correlations. This operation is similar to the scatter diagram, except the latter identifies correlations between different characteristics. Autocorrelation charts are useful during the measure, analyze, and control stages. In the measure stage, these charts may be used to gather information about processes, including their effects on baseline data. During the analyze stage, autocorrelation charts are used to investigate the regression residuals, namely to test for independence. In the control stage, autocorrelation charts are used to develop a strategy that takes into account a process' serial dependence.

Process

The first step of the autocorrelation function is testing for autocorrelations between each of the isolated observations. Each step will be considered in relation to the steps immediately before and after it. This consideration is called the lag 1 autocorrelation. There also will be autocorrelations for distances. For example, the lag 3 autocorrelation will consider the relations between the first and fourth observations, second and fifth observations, and so on. The general recommendation suggests testing for autocorrelations from lag 1 to lag $n/4$, where n is the total number of observations. The estimation of the autocorrelation function for lag m is as follows: $r_m = \frac{\sum_{i=1}^{n-m}(X_i - \bar{X})(X_{i+m} - \bar{X})}{\sum_{i=1}^{n}(X_i - \bar{X})^2}$, where n is the total number of observations and $\bar{X}$ is the average of these observations.

Process partial autocorrelation

The formula for estimating the partial autocorrelation function is $\Phi_{mm} = \frac{r_m - \sum_{j=1}^{n-m} \Phi_{m-1,j} r_{m-1}}{1 - \sum_{j=1}^{m-1} \Phi_{m-i,j} r_j}$, for a given lag of m. In this formula, the autocorrelation function is r_m. The significance limits for both the autocorrelation function and the partial autocorrelation function (if the true population of the ACF or PACF is zero) is calculated at the stated significance level. However, if the true population of the autocorrelation function or partial autocorrelation function is larger, then the significance limit must be determined with $r, \Phi = \pm\left(\frac{k}{\sqrt{n}}\right)$, in which n is the number of observations and k is the ordinate of the normal distribution at the stated significance level.

Interpretation of autocorrelation charts

When interpreting an autocorrelation chart, one should be aware of phenomena that might produce false correlation. For instance, sometimes autocorrelation will be significant only at adjacent data points, where the lag is very low. To diminish this autocorrelation, one should increase the time between data point collection. Another source of false correlation emerges with sampling from several different streams in a process. Sometimes large autocorrelations for smaller lags can influence larger lags. For example, if a strong correlation exists between observation four and observation five and another strong correlation exists between observation five and observation six, observation four and observation six may appear correlated even when no such correlation actually exists. This illusion can be diminished by using the partial autocorrelation function. In any case, autocorrelation functions and partial autocorrelation functions range from -1 to 1. The farther away the value is from zero, the stronger the correlation.

Cause-and-effect diagrams

Cause-and effect diagrams, sometimes known as fishbone or Ishikawa diagrams, are an easy and effective way to depict the reasons for a particular event. The typical layout of a cause-and-effect chart features the causes and effects listed in distinct boxes with arrows pointing from causes to effects. A cause *can* have more than one effect, and an effect *can* have more than one cause. Cause-and-effect diagrams are used during the analyze and improve stages of DMAIC. In the analyze stage, they are used to create innovative lists of possible process factors to be explored further in a designed experiment. In the improve stage, cause-and-effect diagrams are used to create lists of possible failure modes that must be considered when crafting a solution.

<u>Creation and interpretation</u>
The first step in creating a cause-and-effect diagram is making a provisional list of the possible relationships between the process and the outcome. Phrasing the

target in terms of a problem is better than phrasing the problem in terms of a goal. All of the factors that influence a main problem will branch off from that main problem. For some problems, beginning with either the four Ps (people, plants, policy, and procedures) or the 5Ms and E (measurement, material, methods, machines, manpower, and environment) will be appropriate. Using these models can ensure that no significant influences are overlooked. The main causes should be connected to the problem, and subordinate clauses should be connected to the main causes. In especially detailed diagrams, several hierarchical levels of causes may exist. Cause-and-effect diagrams are primarily brainstorming tools, not final assessments, so it is important to include many different possible answers. Once all of the causes and effects have been outlined, the group should examine the diagram to see whether certain categories exhibit a preponderance of causes. These categories may require further subdividing, or they may become targets for problem-solving efforts.

Interaction plots

Interaction plots illustrate the interrelationships of three parameters. In most cases, these parameters are two factors and one response. Interaction plots are used during the analyze and improve stages of DMAIC. In these stages, interaction plots are useful for evaluating the results of designed experiments and multiple regression. Typically, plot variables are placed on the x-axis, and the responses are placed on the y-axis. The distinct lines on the plot are defined by the levels of the interaction variable. If the plot variables exhibit no interaction, then the lines basically will be parallel. That is, both plot variables will produce similar trends when combined with the response variable. If the lines are not parallel, however, an interaction likely exists.

Lean metric velocity

Velocity, in lean management, is a metric that indicates the rate at which value is added during a process phase. The calculation of the lean metric velocity is useful during the analyze stage of DMAIC, where it can place cycle time improvement opportunities in order of importance. The basic formula for the calculation of velocity requires dividing the number of value-added steps by the process lead time. Process lead time is calculated according to Little's law, by dividing the number of items in the process by the number of times the process is completed every hour. Of course, objective figures for these variables are not always readily available. Often, initiating a process observation log is helpful before attempting to calculate velocity.

Calculating process velocity

The first step in the calculation of process velocity requires categorizing every task in the process as value-added, non-value-added but necessary (NVA type 1), or non-value-added and unnecessary (NVA type 2). The next step involves measuring the physical distance between the sites of each successive task. Next, the team will use a control chart to predict the average time required to complete each process task. Then the team will use a control chart to estimate the amount of time a customer or employee must wait before beginning each successive step in the process. At this time, the team also should estimate the number of items in each queue. Again, the control chart is the most valuable tool for this purpose. The averages of all these measurements can be added together to obtain the total number of items in the process and the number of times the process is completed each hour. This is all the information required to calculate process lead time. Velocity is calculated by dividing the number of value-added steps by the process lead time.

Usage of velocity data

The calculation of velocity indicates the degree to which a process responds to customer demands. If there is less work in progress, lead times are shorter and velocity is greater. If the lead times are longer, then velocity is slower. When velocity is slow, the business cannot respond quickly to new orders from customers. For example, if an auto body shop takes a long time to finish working on existing projects, it cannot take on new projects. If the cashier at a grocery store works slowly, the line at his or her aisle likely will grow. The formula for process velocity (number of value-added steps divided by process lead time) suggests a couple of approaches for increasing velocity. Either the amount of work in progress can be reduced or the number of completed processes per hour can be increased. Analysis of process efficiency will indicate which of these strategies is appropriate.

Value stream analysis

The value stream is the entire series of activities that create value in a product or service. The addition value is considered from the perspective of the customer rather than from the perspective of employees or management within the company. During process mapping, the Six Sigma team will divide the activities into three categories: value-added activities, business-value-added activities, and non-value-added activities. Value-added activities, as the name suggests, create value for the customer. Business-value-added (BVA) activities do not create value for the customer, but are necessary anyway. These activities sometimes are referred to as Type 1 waste. Some examples of BVA activities are marketing, design, and delivery. Non-value-added (NVA) activities create value for neither the customer nor the business. The goal of Six Sigma projects is to eliminate as many NVA activities as possible.

NVA activities in the analyze stage of DMAIC

Identification
Six Sigma teams use tools such as matrix diagrams and quality function deployment efforts to identify non-value-added activities. As always, the question of value should be considered from the customer's perspective. If an activity does not create something for which a customer would be willing to pay, it likely does not add value. One common form of NVA activity is improper or unsuccessful designs. When a business spends time and effort designing products or services that the customer ultimately rejects, then the business has failed to add value. If a business process contains some unnecessary or redundant steps, these steps are classified as NVA activities. Any work that does not translate into a product or service for the customer is considered NVA. For instance, inventory reorganization provides nothing to the customer, although it may be necessary at times. Any unnecessary transport of people or resources is considered NVA activity.

Elimination
In the analyze stage of DMAIC, the Six Sigma team will be alert to non-value-added activities that expand cycle time. Non-value-added activities (NVA) create nothing for which a customer would be willing to pay. One common example of an NVA activity that expands cycle time is an authorization requirement. Cycle time extends unnecessarily when an employee must receive permission from his or her superior before moving on to the next step of a processThis unnecessary extension is true especially when the task

has become rote, and authorization is a meaningless formality. Some businesses have implemented checklists requiring employees to complete paperwork at every step in a process. These checklists often are unnecessary and time-consuming.

Batching

Disadvantages
Batching is a traditional method of reducing waste. When work is batched, a specialized group of employees gathers a large number of essentially identical tasks and performs them all at the same time. The group of similar tasks is known as a batch. Throughout most of the modern era of organizational management, batching was considered to make processes more efficient. However, research conducted during Six Sigma efforts has revealed that batching often increases overall cycle time. When process tasks are divided into batches, the time required to perform them clearly is shorter. However, batching creates delays at the beginning and end of the activity. The team must wait for a number of tasks to arrive in the "in tray" before beginning. This wait creates unnecessary lag time. Also, batching typically means that the entire collection of materials does not move on to the next step of the process until everyone has been subjected to the batched step. A product or service may be ready to move on for quite a long time, but may have to wait until the other products or services have been processed.

Benefits
In some cases, batching is a good strategy for processing materials or performing activities. For instance, if the time required to set up the equipment for a particular activity is significant, performing the activity in batches may be more efficient. As an example, consider the process of making soup from scratch.

- 68 -

Even if you are making soup only for yourself, you likely will make much more soup than you can eat in a single sitting, because the time required to gather and manipulate the ingredients is too long to spend on one serving. Without even thinking about it, most people recognize that cooking a large pot of soup is more sensible. Another scenario in which batching makes sense is when the cost of moving materials is large. This scenario occurs often in the shipping of small items. For instance, a business may need only a small number of staples every week, but the cost of shipping office supplies is high enough to suggest that the business should buy large batches of supplies infrequently rather than a small amount of supplies more often.

Seven classic wastes

The Japanese waste-reduction system referred to as *muda* considers seven classic wastes: transportation, inventory, motion, waiting (work-in-progress), over-processing, over-production, and defects. Transportation is a source of waste because moving products and materials risks damaging or losing them. Transportation is not considered a value-added activity. Inventory is considered a waste because it does not contribute to income. Motion is distinct from transportation in that it refers only to the movement of the product during the production process. Waiting, also known as work-in-progress, is defined as the time when goods are neither being processed nor in transport. Over-processing occurs when more work than is necessary is performed on a product. One common form of over-processing is the use of tools or equipment much nicer than the process requires. Over-production occurs when the amount or number of goods produced exceeds the demands of customers. Defects are errors that necessitate reworking or rescheduling.

Muda

The Japanese term *muda* means wasteful or unproductive activity. This term was brought into fashion by the Toyota Production System (TPS), which identified *muda* as one of the three forms of waste, along with *mura* (inconsistency) and *muri* (overburden or overloading). In TPS, the reduction and elimination of muda is considered one of the best ways to increase profits. However, many experts believe that quality engineers have become focused excessively on muda to the exclusion of mura and muri, which means that problems more often are solved through process improvement than through full process redesign. The Toyota Production System identified seven classic sources of waste: transportation, inventory, motion, waiting (work-in-progress), over-processing, over-production, and defects. One of the essential first steps for dealing with muda is to separate waste from activities that add value. Non-value-added activities may be divided further into those activities that are necessary and those activities that are not necessary.

Mura

Mura is a Japanese term meaning unevenness or inconsistency. In the Toyota Production System, mura is one of the three categories of waste. Obviously, the goal of the TPS is to reduce mura, along with muda (unproductive activity) and muri (overloading).The primary means of reducing mura is the implementation of a manufacturing system that avoids excessive inventory and wait times. When processes are continuous and products do not have to wait, less opportunities exist for work to be uneven or inconsistent. A business that has implemented mura will make smaller, more frequent deliveries to customers. Another strategy for reducing mura is to have the same employee perform a few different consecutive tasks during production. This strategy eliminates the possibility that work will become backlogged, since each piece of work will travel with the operator.

Muri

Muri is one of the three types of waste identified by the Toyota Production System. The other two types of waste are muda (unproductive activity) and mura (inconsistency). Muri is defined as overburden, irrationality, or absurdity. In manufacturing, muri exists when processes are organized in the simplest and most repeatable way. One important step in the reduction of muri is the calculation of takt time, or the reasonable allotment of time for each particular task. A manufacturer establishes takt time to obtain a realistic picture of process length. Muri will increase when processes are not standardized and placed in a consistent order. The reduction of muri benefits employee morale because standardized work procedures and sequences inform workers of the expectations placed upon them.

Improve

Basic objectives of the improve stage

The improve stage of DMAIC occurs when all of the hard work of the preceding sections finally is applied to processes. The first major objective of the improve stage is to set the new process operating conditions. These conditions are based on the experimentation and analysis of the measure and analyze phases. The next objective of the improve stage is to identify and address the failure modes for the new processes. Assessing and predicting the benefits of the proposed solution also is appropriate. Before making massive changes, the Six Sigma team should be able to guess how positive the results of these solutions will be. The final objective of the improve stage is to implement and confirm process improvements, the moment when the predictions developed during the preceding sections finally are tested against reality.

Orthogonality

In experimental design, orthogonality is the degree to which the design allows all specified parameters to be measured independently of one another. Orthogonality can be measured by finding the normalized value of the determinant of the information matrix. If an orthogonal design matrix has one row for estimating each parameter, then its measure of orthogonality is 1. A simple check for orthogonality involves adding all the columns in standard format. If the sum of the factor's columns in standard format is equal to zero, then the design is orthogonal. Orthogonality should not be confused with balance in experimental design. A design does not need balance, but it does need orthogonality. For instance, Plackett-Burman and fractional factorial designs typically have both orthogonality and balance. However, if possible, rows can be trimmed from these designs, which diminishes balance but preserves orthogonality.

Tampering

A process is tampered with when it is adjusted in response to variation even though the process itself has not shifted. In short, tampering with a process is responding to a false alarm or treating common-cause variation as if it were special-cause variation. Tampering is more likely to occur when the operator tries to restrict the process to limits inside the natural control limits. As such, tampering can occur when the desired control limits are based on unrealistic goals rather than on statistical data. Tampering also may occur when an operator attempts to place the process within two standard deviations rather than the suggested three. Tampering actually increases variation because it shifts the process in unnecessary directions, thereby generating output significantly less controlled than it should be.

Subsidiary factors

In a designed experiment, subsidiary factors are those factors that contribute to the response and are controlled for the experiment, but are not controlled during the normal iteration of the process. If a subsidiary factor is not included in the design, it will create error in the results. Subsidiary factors may be treated as main factors when they have a strong effect, thereby allowing the interaction effects of the subsidiary factor to be estimated. In some design methodologies, subsidiary factors are synonymous with noise factors. According to Taguchi, for instance, noise factors are those factors that cannot be controlled in real-life operations. Taguchi identified three types of subsidiary factor: external, internal, and unit-to-unit. An external factor is something like dust or vibration that exists outside the operating equipment. An internal factor exists within the equipment, such as aging or material degradation. A unit-to-unit factor depends on variations between processed units. Time of day and material quality are examples of unit-to-unit factors.

Experimental design

In experimental design, subsidiary factors can be difficult if not impossible to control. The best approach often involves setting up operations within a range that minimizes the effects of these factors. This arrangement is called robust design. Estimating the interactions between main and subsidiary factors in an experiment is impossible. Nonetheless, it is possible to include subsidiary factors by constructing a subsidiary design in which the interactions between these noise factors can be estimated. The final design will repeat each run of the main design for each subsidiary design trial, which significantly increases the number of trial runs. Whenever an experiment suggests that the interactions between main and subsidiary factors are influential, it is advisable to run extra trials in which the subsidiary factors are treated as main factors.

Balance in designed experiments

In a designed experiment, two types of balance exist: design balance and data balance. Design balance occurs when the design array has columns with equal numbers of levels for the particular parameter. Data balance, on the other hand, occurs when the data points are distributed in such a way that each point has essentially the same influence on the definition of parameters. A number of designed experiments can achieve both design and data balance. However, central

composite designs emphasize data balance over design balance. Also, in some cases creating an accurate estimate of experimental error is better, which means that more data points should be added. This action can diminish both design and data balance. In other cases, design balance may be sacrificed so the experiment can run in a shorter time frame or with fewer resources.

Blocking factors and casual factors

Blocking factors are necessary when all of the runs in a designed experiment cannot be completed under the same environmental conditions. In other words, all of the factors that can be evaluated in a particular run are placed in a single block and considered together. The block can be only as large as the constraining factor, for instance the number of runs that can be completed in a single day. Blocking factors must not interact with main factors. In the analysis of variance, blocking factors should be considered as random factors. A casual factor, meanwhile, cannot be controlled during the course of the experiment. For instance, if a process occurs outside, the weather would be considered a casual factor. Casual factors also are known as covariates or random variables. Casual factors cannot be included in a design, but they should be recorded. If the data does not fit the model very well, it may be because of an unnoticed but significant casual factor.

Confounding

Confounding is a phenomenon in multiple regressions in which multiple factors cannot be estimated outside of the presence of the other(s). A confounding variable correlates with the independent and dependent variables. In most cases, this occurrence is due an insufficient number of proper runs to derive the required estimates for each of the factors.

If runs are taken out of a designed experiment without an adjustment to the parameter requirements, confounding often results. A couple of types of confounding exist. Operational confounding occurs when a metric intended for one variable measures another variable as well, unbeknownst to the researcher. Procedural confounding occurs when the researcher, through negligence or error, allows another variable to change with the independent variable. Confounding usually can be eliminated by increasing the type and number of comparisons made during the experiment.

Resolution of experimental designs

Design resolution provides information about the types of interactions that can be estimated independently within a particular design. Estimating confounded factors and interactions is impossible. In designed experiments, resolution information is most relevant when complete sets of interactions are necessary. Five main types of resolution exist: III, IV, V, VI, and VII. For first-order models, resolution V and VI designs provide the most of the required detail. Increases in resolution necessitate ever more trials per number of factors. Some designs may be mixed-resolution, if for instance estimates of all the three-factor interactions are not required. This occurrence is typical of response surfaces in which only some factors may generate quadratic effects, and mixture experiments in which the levels of each factor contributes to the whole of the factors.

Resolution III, IV, V, VI, and VII designs

In resolution III designs, one or more main factors may be confounded with an interaction. A resolution III design usually is helpful only as an initial screening measure. In resolution IV designs, main factors are not confounded with two-factor interactions, although they may be confounded with higher-order interactions. Resolution IV designs may have two-factor interactions confounded with one another and with higher-order interactions. In a resolution V design, main-factor and two-factor interactions are not confounded with each other, although they may be confounded with higher-order interactions. Also, in a resolution V design, three-factor and higher-order interactions may be confounded. In a resolution VI design, main-factor and two-factor interactions are not confounded with each other or with three-factor interactions. However, in a resolution VI design, three-factor and higher-order interactions may be confounded with one another. Finally, in a resolution VII design, main-factor, two-factor, and three-factor interactions are not confounded with one another but they may be confounded with higher-order interactions. Also, in a resolution VII design, four-factor and higher-order interactions may be confounded.

Box-Behnken design

The Box-Behnken design is able to cover the experimental space with fewer points than is required for a complete factorial design. This design incorporates a mixture of corner, face, and central points. The Box-Behnken design is like a central composite design, but it does not include any corner or extreme points. Only three-level factors are used, so this design requires no extended axial points. A Box-Behnken design often necessitates a smaller number of runs than a three-level fractional factorial design. Whereas central composite designs often require extreme factor level combinations, Box-Behnken design can avoid these. Unlike other designs, on which factors run at the corner points, the factors on a Box-Behnken design run at the midpoints and the center of the cube.

Central composite design

A central composite design can cover the same number of quantitative factors as a standard fractional factorial design without requiring nearly so many points. In addition, central composite designs are approximately as efficient as standard fractional factorial designs. A central composite design includes corner points, central points, and either extended axial points or face-centered points. If the design includes face points, it must have three levels. This type of experimental design typically is used to map the shapes of the quadratic surfaces in response surface analysis. If the central composite design uses extended axial points, it must have five levels. The position of these axial points, or the levels of the factors, is determined by the desire to have a rotatable design. An experimental design is considered rotatable if the variance of the predicted response is the same at all points the same distance from the design's center.

Complete and fractional factorial designs

A complete factorial design includes every combination of every factor level. The number of runs required by a complete factorial design is completed by raising the number of levels to a power equal to the number of factors. For instance, if a factorial design includes four factors with two levels, the number of runs will be $2^4 = 16$. For obvious reasons, this sort of design quickly can become time-consuming and expensive. In most cases, running a fractional factorial design is better. A fractional factorial design only includes a small subset of the experimental runs required for a complete factorial design. Fractional factorial designs can demonstrate the most crucial features of a problem with much less time and money.

John's ¾ designs

A few obscure factorial designs can be used to save even more time and money than can be saved with a fractional factorial design. A John's ¾ design is an experimental design run at ¾ of the regular fractional factorial design. A common John's ¾ design could include 12 runs (i.e., ¾ of 16) or 18 runs (i.e., ¾ of 24 runs). These designs often are used after a fractional factorial design, when certain interactions need further exploration. Sometimes, though, using this design at the beginning of experimentation is acceptable. In most cases, a John's ¾ design can accommodate more interactions than a fractional factorial design or Placket-Burman design with the same number of runs.

Mixed-level designs

In a mixed-level experimental design, not every factor has the same number of levels. Some mixed-level designs include numerous factors, none of which have the same number of levels. These designs are functional because they incorporate pseudo-factors, or standard values inserted for missing levels in order to obtain values for the other factors at that level. Calculating the number of runs for a mixed-level design requires a slightly more sophisticated operation than for complete factorial designs. For example, if a mixed-level design has three factors with four levels and two factors with two levels, the total number of runs is calculated $3^4 + 2^2 = 81 + 4 = 85$. This number of runs estimates each potential factor and interaction possible.

Plackett-Burman designs

One of the more useful screening designs is the Plackett-Burman design, typically generated in steps of four runs and extending from around four to a hundred runs. The number of runs must be at least

- 74 -

one more than the number of parameters. If it necessary to estimate twelve parameters, then a Plackett-Burman design can do this in only thirteen runs. A Plackett-Burman design will be the same as a standard fractional factorial design when the number of runs is a power of 2 (e.g. 2, 4, 8, 16). The Plackett-Burman design is more efficient than the fractional factorial when the number of runs is equal to a factor of 4 (e.g. 4, 8, 12, 16, 20, 24). However, a ¾ design often can accommodate more interactions for the same number of runs.

Replicated designs and screening designs

In a replicated design, either all or almost all of the main factor design is repeated a few or several times. This process of replication makes it possible for variance to be estimated on every run of the main factor design, which means that an analysis of variance may be performed over the full range of the experiment. A screening design has a small number of runs and is used at first to identify issues that should receive more attention in future experiments. The typical purpose of a screening design is to eliminate factors from subsequent designs. A screening design does not estimate interactions. Plackett-Burman designs, both regular and irregular, are common for screening. A screening design must satisfy resolution III (one or more main factors may be confounded with an interaction) and resolution IV (main factors are not confounded with two-factor interactions but may be confounded with higher-order interactions; two-factor interactions may be confounded with each other and with higher-order interactions).

EVOP strategy

Evolutionary operations (EVOP) most often are used during the analyze and improve stages of DMAIC. In the analyze stage, these strategies are used to assess the significance of various process factors. In the improve stage, these strategies are used to set new process factor specifications. One problem with evolutionary strategies is that they require a great many repetitions in order to isolate the effects of changes in factor levels. EVOP strategies usually take much longer than other designed experiments, and in some cases it may take months before the significance of process changes can be identified. However, productive operations may continue even while an evolutionary operations strategy is being implemented, which is not the case for designed experiments. Also, evolutionary operations strategies assess the process as currently performed, which means that any significant factors overlooked in a designed experiment automatically will become part of the system.

Creation
Evolutionary operations strategies assess performance on a cycle-by-cycle basis. For the purposes of EVOP, a cycle is defined as an interval in which data has been collected at each point in the process design. In evolutionary operations, several cycles are observed and then the experimental conditions are varied. Each set of cycles performed with the new operating conditions is called a phase. The difference between the edge points and the center point is called the change in the mean, or curvature. When implementing an evolutionary operations strategy, limiting adjustments to two or three factors is best. Otherwise, the experiment will be too complicated. The adjustments should be minor so their effects can be observed with precision. The best way to proceed with the experiment for two or three factors is to run it twice before estimating error and the effect significance. If the factor continues to be significant after three cycles, the next phase of the strategy

should be performed with the conditions centered on the new optimal condition. If factors do not appear statistically significant, increasing the range of levels for these factors may be useful.

Redefining process flow

One way to improve processes is to redefine the process flows. A process may be simplified or optimized. Redundant steps may be removed, and level-loading techniques may be applied. Many businesses improve processes by reducing set-up times. Whenever process flows are redefined, assessing the impact on quality is important. The critical-to-quality metrics used during the measure stage are useful. Benchmarking is a common approach to redefining process flows. Benchmarking refers to a systematic review of similar or dissimilar processes in another organization. Too often, benchmarking is assumed a prelude to imitation. People incorrectly believe that benchmarking means mapping out a competitor's process and then copying it. Instead, businesses should use the information they obtain as inspiration.

Simulations

Many Six Sigma teams use simulations to inform their choices during the improve stage of DMAIC. A simulation is a cheap way to predict the likelihoods and effects of variable levels. Simulations can confirm the solutions derived from analysis and can indicate the possible interactions between variables. Simulations are useful for evaluating changing situations because the dynamics of the change can be built into the simulation. Simulations require a process model and a rough probability distribution for every variable. The simulation takes these distributions and creates a resulting frequency distribution. Simulations can be very informative, but they must be confirmed against hard data before or

after they are run. Although simulations are not fool-proof method of research, they certainly are valuable relative to their cost.

Adjustment of operating conditions

During the improve stage, the Six Sigma team must identify or predict optimal operating conditions. This action can be difficult when many input factors contribute to performance. The overarching goal of adjusting operating conditions is to establish levels that provide satisfactory results with minimal variation. If the process model is complex, the best way to identify optimal operating conditions is with response surface techniques. These techniques narrow the regions in which optimal factor settings may occur. Another way to find the best operating conditions is with evolutionary operations, or EVOP. One advantage of EVOP is that it can be implemented as the process continues to run. Changes are made to the process in action instead of in an experimental condition.

Evaluation of process failure modes

The initial goal during the improve stage of DMAIC is to optimize the process flow. Once this optimization is complete, the team will evaluate the new failure modes. In other words, the team will now examine the new operating conditions or process flows for possible sources of deviation. Once these conditions or flows are identified, the team will brainstorm possible solutions. These problems and potential solutions often are depicted on a process decision program chart, which looks a bit like a tree diagram. The process decision program chart is a good first step, but it usually must be supplemented by failure modes and effects analysis, or FMEA. A comprehensive FMEA concludes with the generation of a risk priority number (RPN), indicating the influence of a particular failure on overall performance. The team then must develop mitigation or elimination strategies for the most significant potential failures.

Normalization

Normalization is one of the major techniques of transformation. As such, it places all the values on a common range, from -1 to +1. This technique only works when the experimental array is balanced. After normalization, identifying the most important factors and interactions should be easier, as should calculating the significance and the numerical accuracy of the regression. Normalization may make it easier to select factors to keep or discard in subsequent experiments. Qualitative factors need not be normalized, but quantitative factors may be normalized to great effect. Typically, either all or none of the quantitative factors in an experiment are normalized. Normalizing is more effective in linear experimental models, although in nonlinear experiments it may be used to screen out irrelevant factors or interactions.

Response surface analysis

Response surface analysis is a set of techniques for calculating the best response value. Best response value may refer to the best possible result of an industrial process or the best possible admixture of employees for a service response. Response surface analysis is used only during the improve stage of DMAIC. Here, it maps the response surface so the effects of varying certain factors can be predicted. Response surface analysis also is used in the improve stage to find the operating conditions that produce the desired specifications. In general, though, response surface analysis is used to achieve the best possible settings for processes and products. Response surface analysis cannot be begun until a first-order regression model has been created from the critical set of significant factors. The Six Sigma team will use screening designs to develop the critical set of significant factors.

Process
Response surface analysis, as it is typically practiced, has three phases, 0 through 2. Phase 0 is considered a prerequisite phase. In this phase, the team uses screening designs to create a critical set of significant factors. Then, a first-order regression model is created. In phase 1 of response surface analysis, the team will use the steepest ascent methodology to define the operating region at present and identify the direction of maximum response. The first-order regression model created during phase 0 can be very useful at this point, because its scale is great enough to ensure that the data points are affected by first-order effects. Phase 2 of response surface analysis is the application of ridge analysis and a second-order model to locate the optimal conditions at stationary points in a small region. In response surface analysis, a stationary point is defined as anywhere that the slope of the second-order response surface model is zero for each of the factors. Stationary points may be a maximum value, a minimum value, or a "mini-max" value, which is the highest or lowest point in a saddle curve. If the stationary point is significantly outside the data range, it may be used only to obtain direction.

Steepest ascent methodology in phase 1
Phase 1 of response surface analysis is the application of steepest ascent methodology to a first-order regression model. Data points are collected along the steepest path beginning with the design center, or the spot where $(x_1, x_2) = (0, 0)$. The design center is the first test condition. The steepest ascent is

- 77 -

determined by moving β_1 coded units in the x_1 direction for every β_2 coded units in the x_2 direction, where β_1 and β_2 are the coefficients of the x_1 and x_2 terms, respectively. If the changes are sufficiently small, then obtaining a good picture of the response will be possible. Given a specific change in uncoded units for x_1, it will be possible to obtain values for x_2, β_1, and β_2. It also is possible to determine the path of steepest ascent relative to the physical limitations of the system, such as if either x_1 or x_2 cannot proceed beyond a certain point. The local maximum conditions are determined by looking for the point at which the response begins to diminish. Once the local maximum condition has been determined, another experiment is run near this point to obtain a first-order model with centerpoint(s).

Ridge analysis techniques in phase 2
After a first-order model has been conducted near the maximum at the end of phase 1, there should be several redundant runs to estimate lack of fit. When the lack of fit is insignificant, a new path of steepest ascent may be found by adjusting the intervals, starting point, or direction. If the lack of fit is significant and there is curvature, the point likely is close to a maximum, minimum, or mini-max. At this juncture it now is time to begin phase 2 of the response surface analysis: ridge analysis. In this process, a second-order regression model is generated with a central composite design near the optimum. The next step is to create response surface and contour plots for each two factors. Then, identify the stationary point in the response surface and contour plots. Next, predict the response at the optimum using the second-order regression model. Finally, verify the model by gathering new data in the region around the optimum.

Desirability function

For some processes, attaining optimal performance relative to multiple responses may be possible. Response surface analysis can accomplish this goal with overlaid contour plots or desirability functions. The desirability function is an analytical tool for finding the shared optimal point of multiple functions. To perform the desirability function, one must first define each optimal value as a minimum, maximum, or specified target. The degree to which each response obtains its optimum condition is indicated with a d, and the composite of these responses is designated as D, which is calculated as the geometric mean of each response desirability function: $D = (d_1 \times d_2 \times d_3 \times \uparrow \times d_m)^{1/m}$. This composite value is maximized in each case so d values near the maximum of 1 suggest that all responses are within the desirable range at the same time.

Manipulating response and calculating weights in phase 2
If the intention of using the desirability function is to minimize the response, then there must be a specified target value and an upper boundary. The desired value is then calculated
$$d = \left(\frac{\text{response} - \text{upper boundary}}{\text{target} - \text{upper boundary}}\right)^s.$$
If the intention of using the desirability function is to maximize the response, then there must be a specified target value and a lower boundary. The desired value is then calculated $d = \left(\frac{\text{response} - \text{lower boundary}}{\text{target} - \text{lower boundary}}\right)^s.$ If the intention of using the desirability function is to achieve a target value, then that value and the upper and lower boundaries must be defined. If the response falls between the upper boundary and the target, the desirability function should be calculated as in cases where the intention is to minimize the response. If the response falls between the lower boundary and the target, the desirability function should be calculated as in cases where the intention is to

- 78 -

maximize the response. The values for the s and t weights depend on the relative emphasis on the target and the boundary. If the target and boundary are valued equally, then the s and t weights are 1. If the target is more important, then s and t weights can be between 1 and 10. If the boundary is more important, the s and t weights can be between 0.1 and 1.

Interpretation

Response surface analysis generates charts that can be subjected to analysis of variance. For instance, the F statistic can be used to compare the sum of squares variation caused by pure error with the sum of squares variation caused by curvature. If the curvature is significant, the point likely is close to a local maximum, minimum, or mini-max (that is, a stationary point). If the stationary point falls outside the experimental region, then new data must be required so the region can be enlarged. If this is impossible because the data point falls in a region that would be impossible to reproduce, then constrained optimization should be applied to the steepest ascent methodology. If the stationary point is determined to be a mini-max, then constrained optimization techniques must be applied to the steepest ascent methodology. The full results then can be analyzed after axial points are added to the design at the new centerpoint. These axial points are placed on the design at places where they will achieve rotatable orthogonal design. Again, it is necessary to collect new data around the optimal point for the purpose of verification.

Contour plots

Contour plots are composed of groups of curves. Each of these curves is assigned a constant value according to a fitted response. The path of each of these curves relates to values that have been separated at regular intervals. Any additional factors are placed on the chart according to their

mean or some other value. Contour plots are used typically during the improve stage of DMAIC. Specifically, they are used in response surface analysis to estimate the maximum and minimum responses associated with particular ranges of data. If there are only first-order main effects, the contour plot will have parallel lines separated from one another by equal distances. Whenever interactions occur between the responses, the contour lines curve.

Factorial designs

Factorial designs are used in the majority of experiments. They may be either complete factorial designs or fractional factorial designs. Factorial designs are useful primarily during the analyze and improve stages of DMAIC. In the analyze stage, fractional factorial designs are used to identify process drivers and sources of variation. In the improve stage, fractional factorial designs are used along with center points to estimate the effects of curvature. A complete factorial design can estimate the characteristics and interactions of all the factors in an experiment. Complete factorial designs analyze the interactions of more than two factors at a time. A fractional factorial design, on the other hand, only looks at the interactions between two factors at a time. Interactions between more than two factors are known as higher-order interactions. Because a fractional factorial design ignores these interactions, it can be performed more quickly.

Complete factorial designs

The number of runs required for a complete factorial design is calculated by raising the number of levels for each factor to the power equal to the number of factors. For instance, if each factor has three levels and there are four factors, the number of required runs will be $3^4 = 81$. The factorial design will look like a standard table, with each row representing a different configuration of the factors. Since the number of factors exists in an exponential relationship to the levels for each factor, a small increase in the number of factors will result in a huge increase in the number of required runs. For this reason, complete factorial designs quickly can become unwieldy and inefficient. It is often better to begin with a fractional factorial design to identify multi-factor interactions that require more study. Complete factorial designs are seldom used in the business world.

Fractional factorial designs

Fractional factorial designs restrict their focus to the interactions between pairs of factors. They get away with this through a process called aliasing, in which interactions of more than two factors are represented as a single new actor. For instance, a factorial design with three factors will not consider the interaction between factors 1, 2, and 3, but instead will create a new factor (4) representative of this interaction. This enables the factorial design to be comprehensive with far fewer runs. The only problem with this approach is that the effects of factor 4 cannot be estimated independent of the interactions of factors 1, 2, and 3. This is referred to as confounded data. Fractional factorial designs are good for quickly identifying factor interactions that should receive more attention in subsequent experiments.

Kanban

Kanban, a Japanese term roughly translated as "billboard," is a scheduling system that helps businesses make production decisions. The kanban system is based on the operations of a supermarket. The developers of the system noticed that in a supermarket, customers get what they want and the store stocks only what it knows will sell. The developers of kanban decided to treat manufacturing like a supermarket, where each process acts like a customer, selecting the items it needs from inventory and previous processes. One of the chief insights of kanban is that products should not be pushed along from task to task, but instead pulled by the void created by task completion. In other words, when a task is completed, the operator should look to the previous steps for more work. The result of this approach is that inventories are smaller and work is more continuous. In the kanban system, cards are used to indicate demand in subsequent steps of the production path.

Kanban cards and the three-bin-system

Kanban cards indicate when a work station is ready to receive more materials. The card is displayed when the operator needs more products, parts, or inventory to continue his or her work. These cards are displayed in all sorts of ways: in some companies, they are affixed to posts next to each work station, while in other companies they are dropped into empty containers to encourage refilling. Electronic kanban systems now eschew physical cards in favor of computerized alerts. One of the most common forms of kanban is the three-bin system, with containers on the factory floor, in the factory store, and in the supplier's store. Each of these bins will contain a kanban card indicating the product details and other important information. If the factory floor bin is empty, it is returned to the factory store along with the kanban cards. A full bin is then sent from the factory store to the factory floor. This bin includes a kanban card. At this point, the factory store returns the empty bin and kanban card to the supplier's store. Finally, the supplier returns a full bin to the factory store accompanied by a kanban card.

5S

5S is a lean tool whose name is derived from a set of Japanese words related to organizational hygiene: organization, purity, cleanliness, discipline, and tidiness. For the purposes of American audiences, these words are sometimes translated as sort, straighten, shine, standardize, and sustain. 5S is used most often during the improve stage of DMAIC. Here, it is a valuable strategy for reducing cycle time that does not add value and that is lost to movement, finding lost materials, and inefficiently using the physical space. 5S may also be used to accelerate inventory processes and to diminish accidents in the workplace. The program is implemented according to a five-level system. At the first level, the organization has not been subjected to lean management processes. By the time the fifth level is reached, maximum efficiency and minimum waste have been achieved. In Six Sigma, the data collected according to such a rating system often is placed on a radar chart, which indicates the strengths and weaknesses of each department.

Error-proofing strategies

Error-proofing, often referred to with the Japanese term *poka-yoke*, is a system for preventing defects in production processes. The poka-yoke philosophy asserts that preventing errors is better than detecting them, so processes should be analyzed rigorously and improved so mistakes occur less often. One form of error-proofing is auto-correction systems, which reflexively adjust to changing external conditions. Another form of error-proofing is an automatic shutdown, which stops a machine or process if conditions for an error exist. A final form of error-proofing is the warning signal, which of course depends on the presence of a human operator. Nevertheless, a warning signal can be an effective alert that an error is about to occur. Error-proofing strategies can be expensive to implement and may slow processes at first, but in the long run these strategies will save money and time that would have been wasted on mistakes.

SMED program for reducing cycle time

Six Sigma practitioners always are looking for ways to reduce cycle time. One common target is equipment that must be adjusted or refitted between tasks. The single-minute exchange of die (SMED) program is a classic example of one strategy for reducing this time, known as changeover. This program for reducing changeover time was developed by Shingo. It begins by classifying all activities related to the changeover as internal or external. The machine is stopped during internal changeover time, while external changeover time includes all preparatory activities during which the machine may remain operational. After classification, these activities are placed on a flow chart, and the Six Sigma team considers whether any internal activities can be made external. The goal of SMED is to accomplish as much preparation as possible while the machine is still in operation.

Setup time

As part of their efforts to reduce cycle time, businesses often will target the time required to set up and prepare for activities. Six Sigma defines setup time as the interval between the completion of the last item in the sequence and the beginning of the next item. Setup time consists of four components: preparation, replacement, location, and adjustment. Preparation is the set of tasks necessary to gather all of the materials and people for the activity. Replacement is the set of tasks required to adjust and reconfigure equipment before the next item can be processed. For instance, a printer occasionally will need a new batch of paper loaded before it can continue operation. Location, with regard to NVA activities, refers to the positioning or moving tasks that must be completed between iterations of a process. Adjustment is the set of monitoring or fine-tuning tasks that must be performed between iterations to ensure correct performance of a process.

Reducing preparation time
Preparation time is considered a non-value-added activity and therefore should be reduced as much as possible. Preparation is defined as the set of tasks required to collect and store materials and resources before a process can begin. As such, this set of tasks could refer to the collection of resources from a warehouse or the loading of a computer program. In any case, a few common strategies in Six Sigma reduce preparation time. One of these strategies involves keeping all supplies and equipment as close as possible to the workstation, so employees do not waste time in transit. Another strategy for reducing preparation time groups employees from different departments in work cells. In a work cell, each employee is trained and responsible for a different part of the process. Therefore, the entire operation can be completed without moving the work-in-progress. A final strategy for reducing preparation time is leaving equipment on and ready to go even when not in use.

Reducing time spent on relocation and replacement
Six Sigma professionals view moving and replacing equipment and resources prior to a process as non-value-added activities, which therefore should be minimized. One strategy for reducing time lost due to location issues is standardizing setups. For instance, if a bakery produces a number of different goods, baking them at many different temperatures is inefficient. As much as possible, the bakery should keep the oven at the same temperature and instead vary the amount of time each item bakes. A good strategy for reducing replacement tasks is simplifying the setup protocol, altogether. Too often, businesses create elaborate setup checklists appropriate for new employees but unnecessary for employees familiar with their work. One way to simplify setups is by redesigning fixtures. In addition, having a standard setup procedure for all the members of a product family is helpful.

Reducing adjustment time
As much as possible, Six Sigma professionals reduce the time spent making minor adjustments to equipment and resources before each process iteration. The best way to limit adjustment is to establish good process controls. When a process can be repeated many times in a row in exactly the same way, it will require less adjustment. However, this arrangement may require a fundamental redesign of the process. Six Sigma professionals typically use statistical process control charts and designed experiments to identify those areas of the process that necessitate adjustment. The project efforts then will focus on eliminating or reducing these factors. As always, ensuring that the process components being targeted are on the critical path is essential. If process components being targeted are not on the critical path, then modifications will be pointless.

Value of reducing movement and physical space in processes

The analysis stage of DMAIC often reveals that much time is lost simply moving from one work site to another. Indeed, the most effective strategy for reducing cycle time often involves consolidating the area in which a task is performed. This consolidation enables all the stakeholders in a process to perform their jobs with a minimum of waiting and unnecessary energy expenditure. One common approach to reducing wasteful movement requires grouping employees in multi-function rather than single-function departments. An employee group could include representatives from all of the departments required for the process. When possible, employees can be cross-trained so they are capable of performing several different tasks within a complete process. This practice helps stave off boredom and allows employees to replace one another without interruption of work flow. Businesses that reduce unnecessary movement generally spend less on overhead.

Theory of constraints

The theory of constraints is an approach to improving processes by focusing on their most problematic areas. These problem areas are known as constraints. Even the smoothest processes will have some areas of constraint. Improvement efforts will be devoted to improving performance in this level without sacrificing quality elsewhere. Essentially, the theory of constraints encourages businesses to improve continuously by diagnosing weaknesses and addressing them. There is no end to work under the theory of constraints: once one area has been improved, another becomes the constraint and must be addressed. In order for work to be successful, the business must be able to develop effective strategies for maximizing the potential of the constrained area. This action of maximizing the potential is known as exploiting the constraint.

Measurement of constraints
According to the theory of constraints, a process is only as optimal as its weakest component. When managers use this approach, they must consider processes as interlocking parts rather than as discrete tasks. In most cases, the

constraints are found to result from bad policies rather than bad equipment or employees. Rather than focusing on net profit, cash flow, and return on investment, the theory of constraints emphasizes three measures of system performance: throughput, inventory (or investment), and operating expense. These variables are easier to relate to operations. Throughput is calculated by subtracting the total variable costs of production from the total sales revenue. Inventory is calculated as the total amount of money a business invests in items to be sold, and operating expense is the amount of money required to transform inventory into throughput. These variables can produce values for the other common business metrics. Return on investment can be calculated by subtracting operating expense from throughput and dividing by inventory. Net profit can be calculated by subtracting operating expense from throughput. Finally, cash flow can be calculated by finding net profit and then either adding or subtracting the change in inventory, depending on whether the change has been positive or negative.

First three steps
The application of the theory of constraints consists of five basic steps: identify, exploit, subordinate, elevate, and begin again. The first step, then, is to identify the system's constraint: that is, the weakest link in the chain of tasks. The business must determine whether the constraint is internal, arising from a bad policy or resource, or external, caused by an inefficient market or a bad supplier. The business then must consider whether it will be easy to improve this constraint, and devise a strategy for doing so. The second step is to exploit the constraint, or get the best possible performance from it without additional investment. All of the improvements should be based on operational changes. The third step is to subordinate all other operations to the

- 83 -

implementation of the decision made in step two. In other words, at this point the business should focus exclusively on optimizing the constraining process. The system constraint possibly could be broken by subordination, in which case it is necessary to return to the first step.

Final two steps

The fourth step, elevate, occurs when the business seeks other ways to increase the capacity of the constraining task. If the constraint is internal, for instance, the business might elevate it by purchasing more or better machines or by assigning more employees to the task. The fourth step should break the constraint, if it was not broken already during the subordination step. After completing elevation, the business should return to the first step and identify the new constraints on the system. That is, once the original constraint has been broken, the business will look for the next drag on production. The second constraint to be handled might not be the second-largest constraint in the original identification process; the relative severity of constraints may be affected by the optimization of the primary constraint.

Production leveling

Production leveling, a strategy for reducing waste, is one of the central techniques in the Toyota Production System. A production system is described as level (or smooth) when intermediate goods are produced at a constant rate, enabling subsequent production to be constant and efficient as well. One goal of production leveling is to make processes consistent so all employees will act in harmony. Production leveling minimizes the negative consequences of demand amplification in which small fluctuations in productivity at the beginning of the line become large fluctuations later on. One way to prevent fluctuations is to process small batches only. This method enables

each work station to make small adjustments that keep production smooth. As long as the demand from customers is steady, production leveling is fairly easy to accomplish. However, when customer demand is subject to variation, businesses may opt to use either the demand leveling or production leveling approach. In demand leveling, the business tries to make customer orders more regular and predictable. In production leveling, the focus is on either the volume or the product mix.

Production leveling may be approached from the perspective of either product or volume. Leveling by product means adjusting the product mix or sequence to eliminate inefficiencies. As such, production leveling often is accomplished by means of a heijunka box, a visual scheduling tool that depicts the jobs lined up for production and the times at which they will be completed. In leveling by volume, on the other hand, demand is smoothed by manufacturing at the level of long-term average demand rather than at the precise level dictated by current orders. When this is done, the business must maintain at least enough inventory to cover the difference between the average demand and the maximum possible demand. Carrying this excess inventory is undesirable, but maintaining a constant production level makes it possible to achieve continuous production.

Implementation and verification of changes

For many Six Sigma professionals, the implementation of changes during the improve stage of DMAIC is the most exciting part of a project. At this point, the solutions crafted by the team finally are realized. Communication and documentation must be constant at this point so any problems can be identified and resolved. It may be useful to receive explicit authority from the sponsor before making changes so other employees recognize the importance of buy-in. In any case, participating employees should be given comprehensive instructions and should be monitored closely during the initial phases of implementation. In the best case scenario, the first results will verify the wisdom of the solution and will generate sufficient data for statistical analysis. Once the process can be confirmed as stable and acceptable, it can be enshrined as the new method of operation.

Demand leveling

Demand leveling is one approach to smoothing production processes. It is necessary when customer demand fluctuates. The intention of demand leveling is to make customer demand more regular and predictable. Demand can be leveled in a few different ways. One way to level demand is to adjust the ordering process. For instance, Toyota gets its Japanese customers to agree in general terms before negotiating on specifics. In other words, the basic order enters the production system with plenty of time to spare. Another way to level demand is to evaluate ordering systems. In many cases, ordering patterns that appear to fluctuate wildly actually are quite stable when viewed from a greater distance. A third and final way to level demand is to keep a supply of finished goods on hand to accommodate spikes in the number of orders. This method is unpopular because it requires carrying excess inventory.

Efforts to prevent human error

A Six Sigma team will work to minimize the chances and significance of human error in processes. The typical approach involves dividing human error into three categories: willful, technique, and inadvertent. Willful errors are made on purpose by disgruntled employees. For obvious reasons, they can be difficult to predict and stop. The best way to diminish willful errors is to keep employees happy. Technique errors occur because employees are poorly trained or don't understand processes. Technique errors are not made on purpose, and sometimes they are committed without the employee's awareness. In most cases, technique errors are limited to a particular task or employee. Inadvertent errors are the normal variations that occur in any human endeavor. An inadvertent error happens rarely but cannot be eliminated entirely as long as a person is performing the task. Automating the process is one way to eliminate these errors. Another way to minimize inadvertent errors is to conform the workspace to the physical dimensions of the person so movements are more natural.

Prediction of benefits

The Six Sigma team must justify their proposed solutions by predicting the benefits to be obtained. First, the team may need to use a prioritization matrix to show how proposed solutions are aligned with the most pressing needs of the business. A common metric for proposed solutions is earnings before interest and taxes (EBIT), although this metric requires fixed and variable cost figures. EBIT is calculated by multiplying volume by the difference between price per unit and variable cost per unit and then subtracting fixed cost. When a proposed solution has varying benefits over time, these benefits can be evaluated with net present value analysis. Furthermore, some teams calculate the internal rate of return if the net present value is invested. These sophisticated methods allow the team to determine the probabilities of achieving various levels of savings or profit.

PERT analysis

Program evaluation and review techniques (PERT) analysis is used to estimate the time required by various processes. Furthermore, PERT is an essential part of scheduling and cycle time analysis in which hard data on the duration of certain process steps may be unobtainable. PERT analysis uses probability techniques to determine a best guess about durations. PERT analysis is used during the define, analyze, and improve stages of DMAIC. In the define stage, PERT analysis is used to identify the steps in a process with the most influence on the overall duration of the process. In the analyze stage, PERT analysis is used to determine the critical path of a process cycle. During the improve stage, PERT analysis is used to confirm improvements in the cycle time.

Process

The first step in program evaluation and review techniques (PERT) analysis is to isolate activities on the critical path. This isolation can be done with any number of charts, such as an activity network diagram. For the purposes of PERT analysis, it should be assumed that activity times follow a β distribution. The estimated duration of each activity therefore is calculated with the formula $\mu = (a + 4m + b)/6$, in which a is an optimistic estimate of the time, b is a pessimistic estimate of the time, and m is the most likely time. The calculation for estimated standard deviation for each activity is calculated with $\sigma = b - a/6$. The central limit theorem suggests that the total time for all tasks should be in a normal distribution. Adding up the times for the tasks on the critical path yields a measure of total time. The upper predicted limit for total time is equal to the total time + 1.96 × standard deviation. The lower predicted limit for total time is equal to the total time − 1.96 × standard deviation. These are good estimates for the best and worst possible durations.

Level loading

Level loading is one of the more common lean tools. Its purpose is to regulate and moderate the flow of orders in a particular process. Level loading typically is performed during the improve stage of DMAIC. Specifically, this tool can be useful for diminishing the need for inventory checks during a process. Before level loading can be implemented, protocols must be standardized and employees must be trained in multiple areas. The first step in level loading is to calculate the takt time, or the target process time. This calculation should equal the demand divided by the amount of time available. Takt time should be posted at the work station, and resources should be aligned with it. When variations in demand exist, needs for increased resources also will exist. The intention of level loading strategies is to eliminate wait time at the beginning of processes. Each completed unit should begin the next phase of the production process immediately. There should be a protocol in place for adjusting resources to meet the natural fluctuations in demand.

Control

Preventing deviation

Statistical process control

In Six Sigma, it is preferable almost always to prevent mistakes then to correct mistakes that already have occurred. Detection after the mistake is more expensive, time-consuming, and difficult. Six Sigma teams find the inputs that lead to process variation. If the inputs are controlled, variations and errors can be minimized and even eliminated. Statistical process controls monitor the stability of input and output variables, although this process is more effective at monitoring inputs. If the process capability index C_{pk} is 1.5 or more, then a control chart may be used to assess the Six Sigma-level outputs are good enough. Statistical process control is one of the three common methods for controlling processes: the other two are engineering process control and operational procedures.

EPC

Engineering process control (EPC) is a mechanical system for automatically adjusting input in reponse to process variations. A refrigerator is equipped with a basic engineering process control: when the temperature inside rises too far from the desired level, a cooling engine lowers the temperature. The engineering process control devices used in industry are much more complicated. They can function with multiple inputs and outputs. When engineering process control devices are used, however, one cannot also use statistical process control charts, because the constant adjustment of the EPC system will influence the data. In other words, when engineering process control devices are used, the data collected from the process is not independent.

Operational procedures

Operational procedures are similar to engineering process control, except that humans, rather than machines, execute operational procedures. For this reason, operational procedures are subject to more errors. Still, in some cases, operational procedures still will be the best and cheapest option, especially in transactional processes. One common operational procedure is standardizing the process. For instance, the tellers at a bank could be taught to process deposits according to the same steps every time. Another operational procedure is separating orders by type. Many businesses streamline their responses to orders by dividing orders into several key categories. Another way to prevent deviation with operational procedures is establishing processes for diverting resources when needs are urgent. Operational procedures require careful observation and should be documented on process maps, flowcharts, or written summaries.

Standardizing new methods

The first task of the control stage is standardizing the new methods. The new protocols and processes should be in continuous improvement, but the advances made thus far should be written as policy. Too often, employees fall back into old and unproductive habits after the main thrust of the Six Sigma project is complete. One way to prevent this backsliding is to use process control to monitor process variation. One way to do this is to define the methods of control with a control plan. Another way involves writing out all process procedures and duties on process maps, flowcharts, and sets of work instructions. Process variation always should be monitored with process control. Finally, all employees should receive training in the new methods, and new employees should receive a comprehensive orientation.

Merits of process simplification

One of the most common strategies in Six Sigma involves simplifying needlessly complex processes. When the same process is used to create a wide variety of products and services, the process probably is too complicated. As much as possible, businesses should try to limit the variation in deliverables so processes can be standardized more effectively. When customers have more choices, cycle time tends to be longer. Another way to simplify processes involves restricting sales to a single type of customer. By focusing on a particular customer demographic, a business can preclude frequent requests for variation. One positive effect of reducing process complexity is that inventory levels can be diminished. If fewer modifications or customizations are performed during the creation of a product, fewer spare parts will be required as well.

Rational subgroups

In a typical control chart, rational subgroups are required for an estimation of the short-term process variation. For example, rational subgroups are an integral part of the individual-X and X-bar charts. If short-term variation can be estimated, then this estimation can be used to predict the longer-term variation defined by the control limits. A rational subgroup must be comprised of independent observations. Chemical, service, and discrete part manufacturing processes often are autocorrelated, meaning that variation within each subgroup will be much smaller than variation between different subgroups. Rational subgroups may not contain autocorrelated samples. Rational subgroups also must be comprised of rvations from one stable process.

Subgroups that contain observations from multiple process streams will have a large amount of variation within each subgroup, although the variation between subgroup averages will be relatively smaller. The final criterion for a rational subgroup is that it must be comprised of observations taken in a time-ordered sequence. The observations in the subgroup must depict a process over a short amount of time.

Control plans

A control plan is a general summary of the detection and/or prevention strategies used to control processes or materials. Control plans most often are used during the control stage of DMAIC. They are used to create a record of the strategy used to control the key process variables. A control plan generally is compiled from the results of designed experiments and failure modes and effects analysis. This latter analysis is important because it indicates the most important sources of failure to control. The characteristics that need to be monitored and controlled will be listed along the left side of the control chart. For each characteristic, there will be a specification, measurement technique, sample size, sample frequency, analytical tool, and reaction protocol.

<u>Basic components</u>
Control plans list all of the information related to error prevention and detection efforts. This information is based on designed experiments and failure modes and effects analysis. These processes indicate the processes and inputs that need to be monitored and controlled. The risk priority number generated during FMEA designates the most important failure modes in a process. A comprehensive control plan includes basic information such as the specification related to each relevant characteristic. On a control chart, the

specification is the objective range within which the characteristic tolerably can fall. The control chart also should indicate how the characteristic will be measured and how many measurements will be included in each sample. A control chart also should indicate how often samples will be obtained and the analytical tool with which they will be evaluated. Finally, a complete control chart will include the reaction rules, the response protocols when the characteristic does not meet the specifications.

Listed information

A control plan typically provides six pieces of information for every characteristic: specification, measurement technique, sample size, sample frequency, analytical tool, and reaction protocol. The specification defines what is considered acceptable and unacceptable for this characteristic. It should be expressed as an objective value. For instance, the specification for an oven might be 400 degrees if it needs to be at this temperature in order to function properly. The measurement technique is the equipment and protocol for assessing the specifications. The sample size is the number of measurements required at every collection time. The sample frequency indicates the interval between each successive data collection. The analytical tool is the system for analyzing the measurements. For instance, some characteristics will be monitored with control charts, so any adverse trends can be detected. Finally, the reaction protocols on a control plan will be the directions for employees in the event that a characteristic requires adjustment.

Statistical process control charts

Statistical process control charts use past performance to predict future variations. These charts can confirm the stability of a process. Statistical process control charts are used during the measure, analyze,

improve, and control stages of DMAIC. In the measure stage, they convert common-cause variation into objective data that can be used to baseline processes. Also, statistical control charts can be used during the measure stage to evaluate the repeatability and reproducibility of a measurement system. In the analyze stage, statistical control charts can be used to distinguish common and special causes of variation. In the improve stage, statistical control charts can be used to confirm the success of process improvements. Finally, in the control stage of DMAIC, statistical control charts can be used to confirm the stability of adjusted processes and to confirm that the adjustments have improved the process.

Creation

All control charts hold certain characteristics in common. First, the x-axis value must be sequential on every chart. Often, time is plotted along the x-axis. The y-axis, on the other hand, will be for the statistic being charted for each unit on the x-axis. Also, a statistical process control chart will define limits for the plotted statistic. Control limits are calculated by observing process behavior. In order for a control chart to work, it must be derived from rational sub-groups (samples), or short-term variation will not indicate long-term variation. A sub-group is considered rational if the causes of within-subgroup variation are approximately the same as the causes of between-subgroup variation. In other words, any observed variation should be random. Each subgroup will indicate the current location in the process and the amount of variation at that location.

Required calculations for range and sigma charts

The plotted statistic for a range chart is calculated as follows: $\text{Range}_j =$

$\max(x_1, x_2, \dots, x_n) - \min(x_1, x_2, \dots, x_n)$. The centerline is the average range. The upper control limits are calculated $\text{UCL}_R = \bar{R} + 3d_3\sigma_x$ and the lower control limits are calculated $\text{LCL}_R = \max(0, \bar{R} - 3d_3\sigma_x)$. In these equations, $\bar{R}$ is the average range, d_3 is a function of n, and σ_x is process sigma. In the calculation of process sigma, the average range is set as $\bar{R}/d_2$. In a sigma chart, the plotted statistic is the subgroup standard deviation,

calculated $S_j = \sqrt{\dfrac{\sum_{i=1}^{n}(x_i - \bar{x}_j)^2}{n-1}}$, where x_i are the observations in subgroup j, $\bar{x}_j$ is the subgroup average for subgroup j, and n is the subgroup size. The centerline of the sigma chart is the average sigma. The upper control limits are calculated $\text{UCL}_S = \bar{S} + 3\left(\dfrac{\bar{S}}{c_4}\right)\sqrt{1 - c_4^2}$, and the lower control limits are calculated $\text{LCL}_S = \min\left[0, \bar{S} + 3(\bar{S}/c_4)\sqrt{1 - c_4^2}\right]$, where $\bar{S}$ is the average sigma and c_4 is a function of n.

P charts

P charts are a type of control chart primarily used for attributes data. A P chart measures the percentage of samples with a particular characteristic in situations where sample size may vary and the sample unit either will have the characteristic or not have the characteristic. P charts are used during the measure and improve stages of DMAIC. In the measure stage, they are effective at estimating the process baseline from the attributes data. However, using a variables control chart in this capacity generally is preferable. In the improve stage, P charts are used to estimate the number of errors. Like Np charts, however, they are not ideal for this purpose because of the low number of errors. P charts can be generated by Minitab, Excel, and other statistical software programs.

Creation

When creating a P chart, it is important to gather the samples from the same point in the process every time. Unlike an Np chart, in which the samples must have the same number of units, a P chart can be constructed from samples with varying numbers of units. For a P chart, the plotted statistic is the percentage of items in each sample that have the target characteristic. The plotted statistic is calculated $p_j = \dfrac{(\text{count})_j}{n_j}$, where n_j is the number of units taken from group j. The centerline is calculated with $\bar{p} = \dfrac{\sum_{j=1}^{m}(\text{count})_j}{\sum_{j=1}^{m} n_j}$. Again, n_j is the sample size of group j, and m is the number of groups included in analysis. The upper control limit is calculated with $\text{UCL} = \bar{p} + 3\sqrt{\dfrac{\bar{p}(1-\bar{p})}{n_j}}$, and the lower control limit with $\text{LCL} = \max\left[0, \bar{p} - 3\sqrt{\dfrac{\bar{p}(1-\bar{p})}{n_j}}\right]$. In both of these equations, $\bar{p}$ is the average percent.

Interpretation

On a P chart, all of the data points should lie between the upper and lower control limits. In such a case, the process is said to be in statistical control. As long as the data points remain within the control limits, any variation may be attributed to common causes. If all the data points are within the control limits, the process is said to be within statistical control and future performance can be predicted. However, if data points lie outside of the control limits, this must be blamed on special causes of variation. The next step for the Six Sigma team will be to consider possible sources of special-cause variation and then measure them with designed experiments. Even when a P chart contains some points outside the control limits, it is possible to predict the future process capability by simply removing the out-of-control points.

C charts

A C chart is a type of control chart appropriate for attributes data. A C chart tracks the number of events in a sample of a predetermined size. The distinguishing feature of a C chart is that the measured event may occur more than once in each unit of the sample. For instance, a C chart may be used to track errors in a particular process, with the knowledge that several errors might occur in a single iteration of the process. C charts typically are used during the measure and improve stages of DMAIC. During the measure stage, C charts are used to estimate process baselines with attributes data. IT may be better, however, to use a variables control chart for this purpose. In the improve stage, there may also be a role for the C chart, although hopefully by this point in the process the number of errors will be too small for the C chart to be the most effective.

Creation
Creating a C chart begins with selecting an appropriate sample. The samples must be taken from a specific part of the process at the same time. The important feature of the C chart is that each element of the sample may have more than one of the featured attributes. For instance, if the purpose of the C chart is to measure errors during a particular part of production, each instance of that process may contain more than one error. In a C chart, the plotted statistic is the number of occurrences of a particular event during the sample. The centerline of the chart is determined with the formula $\bar{c} = \frac{\sum_{j=1}^{m}(count)_j}{m}$, where m is the number of groups used in the analysis. The upper control limit of the chart is calculated UCL= $\bar{c} + 3\sqrt{\bar{c}}$, and the lower control limit is calculated LCL= $max(0, \bar{c} - 3\sqrt{\bar{c}})$. For both control limit formulae, $\bar{c}$ is the average count and n is the sample size.

X-bar charts

X-bar charts, sometimes called $\bar{X}$ charts, are control charts for variables data. These charts take the averages from subgroups (of observations) to get a view of the process location over time. X-bar charts are most useful during the measure, analyze, improve, and control stages of DMAIC. In the measure stage, they are used to baseline processes by identifying the inevitable amount of common-cause variation. They also are used in this stage to evaluate the repeatability and reproducibility of a measurement system. In the analyze stage, these charts are used to distinguish special and common causes of variation. In the improve stage, X-bar charts are used to confirm that implemented changes have improved the process metric. Finally, in the control stage, X-bar charts are used to ensure that processes remain statistically stable.

Implementation
X-bar charts are useful when subgroups of more than two observations can be measured. The x-axis of the X-bar chart is time, so the chart serves as a chronological model of the process, moving from left to right. Of course, all data entered into an X-bar chart must be assigned a time, or else special-cause variation may not be noticeable. If the size of the subgroup is greater than ten, then a range chart should not be used to monitor process variation, because it will do a poor job of estimating process sigma. Instead, a sigma chart should be used. If the subgroup sizes are 1, an exponentially weighted moving average or individual-X/moving-range chart may be used.

Required calculations
A certain set of calculations are required for an X-bar chart. These charts can be generated by Excel and Minitab. Before an

X-bar chart can be created, the team must determine the appropriate subgroup size and sampling frequency. The plotted statistic for an X-bar chart is the subgroup average. The centerline is the grand average. The upper control limits are calculated $\text{UCL}_{\bar{x}} = \bar{\bar{x}} + 3\left(\frac{\sigma_x}{\sqrt{n}}\right)$, and the lower control limits are calculated $\text{LCL}_{\bar{x}} = \bar{\bar{x}} - 3\left(\frac{\sigma_x}{\sqrt{n}}\right)$. In these equations, $\bar{\bar{x}}$ is the grand average and σ_x is process sigma. Process sigma is calculated with either the subgroup range or the subgroup sigma statistic.

Interpretation

Before interpreting the X-bar chart, one must first examine the range chart. When the range chart is out of control, the control limits on the X-bar chart will not be useful. When the range chart contains points outside of statistical control, the special causes of this variation must be identified and eliminated. Some range charts will have only a few distinct values, suggesting that the chart needs better resolution. After any points outside statistical control have been removed, the X-bar chart may be interpreted relative to control limits and run-test rules. Any points on the X-bar chart outside statistical control must be eliminated. This elimination is accomplished in the usual way: the special causes of variation are identified through brainstorming and data analysis, and the operating conditions are adjusted accordingly.

EWMA charts

An exponentially weighted moving average (EWMA) chart is a type of control chart primarily used for variables data. The creator of the chart selects a weighting factor, which assigns different values to data depending on its age. This type of chart uses data from every available sample, so it can identify extremely small variations in the process.

Exponentially weighted moving-average charts are used during the measure and control stages of DMAIC. In the measure stage, these charts are used to baseline a process. Exponentially weighted moving-average charts are valuable especially for this purpose when the process might be nonnormal and the rational subgroup size is only one. In the control stage, exponentially weighted moving-average charts are used to control the process, either for the reasons outlined in the measure stage or when it is necessary to detect extremely small shifts in the process. Given the same sample size, an exponentially weighted moving average chart can detect shifts from $1/2\sigma$ to 2σ faster than a Shewhart chart.

Creation

One of the most important initial steps in the creation of an exponentially weighted moving-average chart is setting the value for λ (lambda), the weighting factor. To detect small shifts, the value should be set around 0.2; to detect large shifts, the value should be set between 0.2 and 0.4. The plotted statistic for an EWMA is calculated with $z_t = \lambda_1 \bar{x}_t + (1 - \lambda_1)z_{t-1}$, where t is a particular time, λ is the value of the weighting factor, $\bar{x}_t$ is the subgroup average for the present subgroup at t, and the value of z at t_0 is either the overall average or a target. The control limits are calculated with $\text{CL}_{\text{EWMA}} = z_0 \pm \left(\frac{3\bar{R}}{d_2\sqrt{n}}\right)\sqrt{\frac{\lambda}{(2-\lambda)}[1 - (1 - \lambda)^{2t}]}$, where z_0 is the target value or process mean value, n is the size of the subgroup, m is the number of functions being analyzed, and d_2 is a function of n.

Interpretation

The first step in the interpretation of exponentially weighted moving-average charts is to examine the range chart. If this chart is out of statistical control, then the control limits found on the EWMA cannot be trusted. Any points out of statistical control should be linked to special causes of variation. The team may need to think creatively in order to discover the sources of process variation. After the range chart has been reviewed, the EWMA chart may be compared to the control limits. Run tests and specifications are irrelevant in the interpretation of EWMA charts, because process observations will display much broader variation. If the process appears to be stable, then it considering its capability relative to requirements may be useful.

Np charts

The Np chart is a control chart used to assess attributes data. This chart measures the number of times a condition exists in each sample, when the condition may occur only once and the sample size is consistent. Np charts are used during the measure and improve stages of DMAIC. In the measure stage, they use attributes data to guess the process baseline. Whenever possible, however, a variables control chart is used in lieu of an Np chart for this purpose. During the improve stage, Np charts are used to determine the number of errors in process samples. However, the relatively small number of errors in most processes makes the Np chart a somewhat ineffective tool for this purpose. Np charts can be generated on Excel, Minitab, and other statistical software programs.

Creation
To create an Np chart, it is necessary to gather sample data at the same point in each process. Also, every sample should have the same number of units. The plotted statistic is defined as the number of items in the sample that have the particular characteristic. The centerline of the chart is calculated with the following equation: $n\bar{p} = \frac{\sum_{j=1}^{m}(\text{count})_j}{m}$, in which m is the number of groups involved in the

analysis. The upper control limits are calculated with the following formula: $\text{UCL}_{np} = n\bar{p} + 3\sqrt{n\bar{p}(1 - \bar{p})}$. The lower control limits are calculated with the following formula: $\text{LCL}_{np} = \max[0, n\bar{p} - 3\sqrt{n\bar{p}(1 - \bar{p})}]$. In each of the control limit calculations, the sample size is n and the average count is $n\bar{p}$. The value for $\bar{p}$ is calculated $\bar{p} = \frac{\sum_{j=1}^{m}(\text{count})_j}{m \times n}$.

Interpretation
An Np chart depicts a stable process when all of the data points lie between the upper and lower control limits. Any variation within these limits is due to common causes, but any variation that results in data points outside the control limits must be attributed to special causes. Data points that lie outside the control limits must be explained. Typically, an Np chart is succeeded by experimentation aimed at diagnosing particular causes. However, until these special causes of variation have been determined, the capability of the process can be predicted by eliminating the data points that lie outside the control. This elimination will remove the extreme data points from the formulae for average and control limits, which will provide a more reasonable estimate of future performance.

Individual-X and moving-range charts

Individual-X and moving-range charts are control charts used to assess variables data. A moving-range chart depicts changes in variation between consecutive subgroups over an interval. An individual-X chart assesses the process location over an interval using a subgroup with a single observation. Individual-X and moving-range charts are used during the measure, analyze, improve, and control stages of DMAIC. In the measure stage, these charts are used to baseline processes by creating an objective measure of inherent process variations. In the analyze stage, these charts are used to distinguish special and common causes for variation. In the improve stage, these charts are used to confirm the results of improvements. Finally, in the control stage, these charts are used to confirm the stability of improved processes.

Creation of individual-X charts
In an individual-X chart, the plotted statistic is the observation. For a normal distribution, the centerline is the average. For a non-normal distribution, the centerline is the median of the fitted distribution. The upper control limit is calculated $UCL_x = \bar{x} + 3\sigma_x$ and the lower control limit is calculated $LCL_x = \bar{x} - 3\sigma_x$, where σ_x is the process sigma and $\bar{x}$ is the average. When the process is non-normal, the upper control limit is set at the 99.865 percentile of the fitted curve, and the lower control limit is set at the 0.135 percentile. Selecting a distribution curve can be difficult because the control limits are based on the curve, but the curve cannot be set until it is verified that the process is under statistical control. For this reason, many people prefer to use the EWMA or some other chart to establish process control so a distribution can be assigned to the data.

Creation of moving-range charts
In a moving-range chart, the plotted statistic is the moving range, or the difference between the immediate observation and the immediately preceding observation of the sub-groups in an individual-X chart. The moving range is calculated $MR = |x_j - x_{j-1}|$. The centerline is calculated $\overline{MR} = \frac{1}{m-1}\sum_{j-1}^{m} MR_j$, where m is the total number of subgroups and MR_j is the moving range for subgroup j. The upper control limit is calculated $UCL_{MR} = \overline{MR} + 3d_3\sigma_x$ and the lower control limit is calculated as $LCL_{MR} = \max(0, \overline{MR} - 3d_3\sigma_x)$, in which $\overline{MR}$ is the average of the moving ranges, d_3 is a function of n, and σ_x is the process sigma. If a process has a normal distribution, then the moving-range chart will not display any special causes not also displayed on the individual-X chart.

Interpretation
After an individual-X chart is completed, it should be searched for special-cause variation. Any special causes of variation must be identified and removed. During this identification and removal, the future capability of the process can be predicted by eliminating any out-of-control points from the analysis. Special causes of variation should be identified and studied in designed experiments. The general strategy when interpreting individual-X and moving-range charts is to find non-random behavior or trends in the data. One way to find these trends is to apply the run-test rules. Once a process has been observed for a sufficient time and is found to be in control, calculating the process capability relative to requirements is possible. However, it is not possible to predict the capability of a process not in statistical control.

Run-test

Rules
Western Electric created run-test rules as additions to the standard control chart. The purpose of these tests is to identify patterns in the plotted points on a control chart. There are eight run tests in all. All eight of the tests can be used for $\bar{X}$ and individual-X charts. The first four run tests can be used for P, U, Np, and C charts. In run test 1, there is one subgroup with more than three standard deviations from the mean, which suggests a shift in the process mean. Run test 2 has nine consecutive subgroups on one side of the average. In run test 3, six subgroups in a row either increase or decrease. In run test 4, fourteen consecutive

- 94 -

subgroups alternate being greater or smaller than the preceding and succeeding subgroups. In run test 5, two of the three consecutive subgroups are greater than two standard deviations from the mean. In run test 6, four out of five subgroups in a row are greater than one standard deviation from the mean. In run test 7, fifteen consecutive subgroups are within one standard deviation. Finally, in run test 8, eight points in a row are more than one standard deviation from the center.

Typical application

On m and individual-X charts where the normal distribution is used, run tests are applied as they were written in the Western Electric Statistical Quality Control Handbook. On an individual-X chart for which a non-normal distribution has been used, the median is substituted for the average. Also, on these charts, it is necessary to establish zones that produce the same probabilities as the normal curve for the given standard deviation. When applying run tests to the upper and lower halves of a control chart, run tests 1, 2, 5, and 6 should be applied separately. The other run tests (3, 4, 7, and 8) are applied to the entire chart. The option to use run tests is typical of statistical process control programs.

Interpretation

Run tests either identify shifts in the process mean (1, 2, 3, 5, and 6) or provide information about sampling errors (4, 7, and 8). Run test 4 suggests that samples have been taken from a multi-stream process, while run test 7 suggests that sample stratification exists. Run test 8 suggests that samples have been taken from a mixture. Very occasionally, run charts incorrectly may identify errors in the statistical control chart. For the most part, however, these tests are effective at identifying problems in data collection. It should be noted that run tests alert the user to errors but are not as effective at

locating those errors. For many of these tests, a good number of data points must pass through before the run test is activated. Therefore, when a run test is violated the user should go back and analyze the data to discover its location.

TPM

Manufacturers must develop equipment maintenance schedules that maximize production. Too often, maintenance is put off in order for production to continue. Unfortunately, serious malfunctions can occur in which products are damaged or destroyed, and maintenance becomes repair or even replacement. Total productive maintenance (TPM) is a system for optimizing equipment. TPM establishes ways to calculate quality and productivity. According to this model, the three measures of equipment effectiveness are availability, performance efficiency, and the rate of quality products. The overall equipment effectiveness is calculated by multiplying these three factors. Availability is affected by equipment failures and required adjustments and iscalculated by subtracting the amount of time lost to failures and adjustments from the overall available time and then dividing by the overall available time.

Performance efficiency

In total productive maintenance, overall equipment effectiveness is calculated by multiplying availability, performance efficiency, and the rate of quality products. Performance efficiency is the degree to which the equipment operates at maximum speed and capacity. As such, performance efficiency is undermined by idling, stoppages, and reduced speed. Performance efficiency is calculated by multiplying the theoretical (optimal) cycle time by the production amount and then dividing by the operating time. The theoretical cycle time is the interval required to process a standard amount of material. For example, if a machine is capable of processing 2 tons of material every hour, the theoretical cycle time is 0.5 hours/ton. Of course, very few machines approach their theoretical cycle time in practice.

Rate of quality products
In the total productive maintenance system, the overall effectiveness of a piece of equipment is calculated by multiplying its availability, performance efficiency, and rate of quality products. The rate of quality products is the degree to which the equipment avoids errors or defects. The rate of quality products will be lower when reduced yields or process defects are associated with the equipment. The rate of quality products is calculated by dividing the amount of salable product by the total amount of production. For example, if a mill processes 1000 tons of lumber, but only 950 tons are fit to be sold, the rate of quality products is 0.95. If the rate of quality products is extremely low, it suggests that the equipment needs to be repaired or calibrated more often. However, frequent repair and fine-tuning can reduce availability and performance efficiency.

Training

Even when a Six Sigma project is accompanied by massive documentation and comprehensive control plans, employee training is very important for maintaining improvements. Employees should learn the updated processes, of course, but they also should learn the most important process factors and inputs. Sometimes this information will not seem necessary strictly for the performance of the employee's job, but a little context gives the employee a sense of the rationale for changes. Training shows the employee why the process changes will improve his or her work. Training sessions should include

employees from different departments and levels of the organization. However, it training sessions should be pitched to the level of the audience so all employees will understand the content. All training sessions should conclude with some sort of evaluation in order to gauge employee comprehension.

Documentation at the close of the control stage

The final results of the Six Sigma project will be summarized in a project report. This report should begin with the project charter. The report also should include a summary of the results from each DMAIC stage. The report should provide objective indications of whether the short- and long-term goals were met. These objective conclusions should be buttressed with raw data and analysis, which may be included in an appendix to the report. The project report should outline the expenditures and the cost savings related to the project and should outline the control plan designed to keep the project's changes in place. Finally, the project report should include some recommendations or suggestions for future projects in this line.

PICK charts

PICK charts are a lean Six Sigma tool for organizing ideas related to process improvement. Ideas are placed into categories and in order of importance. The name of the chart stands for possible, implement, challenge, and kill. Ideas fall into one of these four categories depending on their perceived payoff and ease. If an idea has a low payoff and is easy to do, it is defined as possible. If an idea has a high payoff and is easy to do, it is defined as something to implement. If an idea has a high payoff and is hard to do, it is designated as a challenge. Finally, if an idea has a low payoff and is hard to do, it is slated to be killed. This simple

chart makes it possible to discern quickly
which ideas are most worthy of
immediate attention.

Design for Six Sigma Frameworks and Methodologies

DMADV and DMAIC

DMADV and DMAIC are both Six Sigma methodologies, but they have different applications. DMADV stands for define, measure, analyze, design, and verify, while DMAIC stands for define, measure, analyze, improve, and control. DMADV is the appropriate methodology for new products and processes because it includes a design phase. Another instance in which the DMADV methodology might be useful is when DMAIC has proven ineffective at bringing an existing process up to sufficient quality standards. If a process needs to be created from scratch or subjected to a comprehensive overhaul, DMADV is appropriate. DMAIC, on the other hand, is suited for gradual improvements of existing processes and products. DMAIC is appropriate for bringing processes and products into alignment with customer requirements and quality standards.

DMADOV

DMADOV (design, measure, analyze, design, optimize, and verify) is a slight variation on the DMADV methodology. Obviously, the main difference concerns the former's extra optimization stage. In optimization, the Six Sigma team employs a range of advanced statistical tools and modes to predict the performance of the design. Optimization is appropriate when the Six Sigma project is aimed at a process that can be accomplished more or less efficiently. The process begins by creating a mathematical description of the process. This description then is used to create a

model into which hypothetical performance specs can be entered. In a complex model hundreds or even thousands of variables may affect this model. By tinkering with the model, the business eventually can obtain an idea of the optimal inputs and settings for the process.

IDOV

IDOV is one of the common methodologies of Six Sigma. It stands for identification, design, optimization, and validation. In the identification phase, the business determines the needs of customers. Also, the business will create an effective business model and establish a Six Sigma team. In the design phase, the team uses critical-to-quality metrics to determine the best methods for processes. In the optimizing phase, the Six Sigma adjusts the factors that contribute to processes until the best outputs are achieved. Finally, in the validation phase, the Six Sigma team makes any necessary changes to the new process. IDOV is the methodology most commonly associated with design for Six Sigma, or DFSS. Unlike DMAIC, DFSS emphasizes defect prevention rather than reduction. Also, DFSS is more concerned with the creation of new, high-quality processes than with the incremental improvement of old processes.

Product DFSS implementation

A design for Six Sigma project can take many forms, but a general path for product DFSS implementation exists. The first step is a meeting between the Six Sigma black belt and champion. At this meeting, the two experts consider the business from a long distance, what is known in Six Sigma as the satellite view. They then will isolate some important metrics and relate them to business needs, with the intention of finding areas in which the existing range of products could be expanded or enhanced. The black belt and champion might brainstorm a list of similar products, so the development processes used in the past can be evaluated. The champion and black belt will generate a set of slightly more close-up metrics, from what is known as the 30,000-foot level. The intention of these measurements is to shift the focus from the developed products to the process of product development. Finally, the champion and black belt will draft a project charter.

After drafting a project charter, the Six Sigma black belt and champion of a typical product DFSS project will devise a strategy for meeting the customer's requirements. Then these experts will create a team of key stakeholders. At this point, the black belt, champion, and stakeholders will have their initial meeting. One of the key items on the meeting's agenda will be the resolution of any issues that could interfere with regular status reporting or the structure of the project. The team will cooperate to produce problem and goal statements. They also will create a SIPOC diagram and a gap analysis of the product development process to customer needs. Using a high-level process map, the team will take a closer look at the development process. The black belt is in charge of ensuring that the selected 30,000-foot metrics are aligned with the satellite-level metrics.

After leading the initial project team meeting, the black belt in charge of a product DFSS project will meet with the finance department. The purpose of this meeting will be to establish the possible business impact of the fledgling project. The finance department should help the black belt outline the financial issues related to the project, and the two parties should agree on appropriate financial metrics. The black belt should make sure that the financial analysis includes an

indication of how the project could reduce costs in the long run. In many projects, the analyses of designed experiment results are useful for predicting the financial benefits of a possible solution. The team then can make a general plan of the project, and if it will be useful, compose a Gantt chart.

After creating a Gantt chart for the new product DFSS project, the Six Sigma team will collect some data from similar projects. In particular, the team will determine the most useful metrics from past product development projects. These metrics should be displayed in time-series format, so the chronological order of previous products is apparent. At this point, the Six Sigma team will create control or run charts of key process output variables (KPOVs) from the 30,000-foot level. Some of the most important KPOVs are return on investment from the product and development cycle time. These control charts should be able to isolate places in which the product development process was affected significantly by special causes of variation. If the products all have responses that lie within the control limits, then any variation is the result of noise during the product development process. All of this work will be based on the business' data records, so an operational archiving program is important.

In a Six Sigma project focused on processes, metrics typically are based on specifications, which in turn are based on customer preferences. This arrangement usually is inappropriate for a product DFSS project, however. For product DFSS, metrics more often are based on long-term capability and performance. In particular, many projects use frequency of occurrence as a primary metric. For instance, a project might determine how often a product development team completes a cycle within a given amount of time (e.g., "70% of development projects are completed in between 6.2 and 7.5 months"). As with all Six Sigma metrics, expressing in monetary terms is important. Once appropriate metrics have been identified, previous products should be evaluated to identify recurrent nonconformance issues. These issues can be plotted on a Pareto chart. These Pareto charts often reveal that what appeared secondary or insignificant problems actually are responsible for severe delays or deviations.

After nonconformance issues are plotted on a Pareto chart, the typical product DFSS project will continue with the creation of a detailed process flowchart or map. This chart or map must be created with sufficient detail to indicate other possible courses of action. The black belt and team also should pay attention to the manner of collecting information about customers as well as the impact of voice-of-the-customer inputs on product development. There should also be some mechanism for identifying issues related to cycle time. Many product DFSS teams find that lean tools such as time-value diagrams and value stream analysis are good for this purpose. In any case, the next step for the project team will be to create a cause-and-effect diagram of the key process output variables. The selection of entries for this diagram will be based on the process flowchart and Pareto chart.

Using their new cause-and-effect diagram, the Six Sigma team then will identify the strength of the relationships between process input and output variables on a cause-and-effect matrix. If the matrix is effective, it will indicate the most important input variables. These input variables then can be ranked on a Pareto chart, thus suggesting the key process input variables. The next step is the creation of a detailed failure modes and effects analysis in which the inputs are

the steps in product development. In some cases, a systems point of view is more appropriate than other points of view. If this approach is used, the input items will be the most significant values in the cause-and-effect matrix. At this point, it assessing the current control plans is appropriate. The failure modes and effects analysis should consider whether the current battery of development tests and measurement systems are risky. Performing a measurement systems analysis might be necessary. This is also a good time to consider applying the theory of inventive problem-solving, designed experiments, DOE collective response capability assessment, or simplified quality function deployment.

After creating and applying the failure modes and effects analysis, the product DFSS team often will gather data from earlier development projects and examine closely the relationships between key process input and output variables. If this task is successful, identifying sources of process variability will be possible. These sources then can be represented visually on multi-vari charts, marginal plots, box plots, and other media. The statistical significance of the relationships between key process input and output variables can be assessed with hypothesis tests. If a great deal of information from previous product development cycles exists, the origins of output variability may be suggested by variance components analysis. Moreover, when significant historical data exists it may be possible to perform analyses of variance, analyses of means, correlation studies, and regressions, all of which may illuminate the influence of KPIVs on KPOVs.

After completing a battery of studies on the statistical significance of KPIVs on KPOVs, the product DFSS team will assess the manufacturing, supplier, and design elements of the development process with response surface analysis, pass/fail functional testing, and designed experiments. Obviously, assessments of the manufacturing elements are necessary only when noticeable variation has occurred in key process output variables during the manufacturing process. For instance, when significant variation in the quality of raw material exists, it might be appropriate to design experiments that identify KPIV adjustments to make the process more resistant to noise. When the current set of reliability tests have done a poor job of predicting product failure rates, applied DOE may prove an effective replacement or addition. Many product DFSS teams conclude that DOE should be implemented as a control methodology in the development process. In any case, designed experiments and other methods can indicate the best operating windows for KPIVs with regard to manufacturing.

After using DOEs and other methods to identify the KPIV operating windows with the best impact on manufacturing, the product DFSS team will update the control plan. During this task, a product development control plan may include pass/fail functional testing methodologies, fractional factorial DOE experiments, and reliability assessments, which all can be important. The control plan also should indicate how the development department (and other departments) will intervene whenever problems occur. Finally, the product DFSS team will verify the process improvements, stability, performance, and capability going forward. The team will gather to create a final project report summarizing the benefits of the project, including the financial benefits. This project report should be disseminated throughout the organization.

Process DFSS implementation

A typical process DFSS implementation begins with the black belt and champion analyzing extremely long-distance metrics, known in Six Sigma as satellite-level metrics. When this analysis suggests a business need to create a new process, then a process DFSS project is warranted. The next step for the black belt and champion is to compose a project charter. This document should include a general plan for project implementation. Around this time, the black belt should indicate the way in which the financial benefits of the program will be calculated. Then, stakeholders are identified and a team is formed. The next step in the Six Sigma project will be to define its customers, whether internal or external. At an initial team meeting, the black belt, champion, and proposed team members will consider a problem statement, goal statement, and a gap analysis of the process to customer needs. The team also will analyze some 30,000-foot-level metrics, and make sure that these metrics align with the metrics obtained from the satellite level.

After aligning the 30,000-foot-level metrics with the satellite-level metrics, the process DFSS project team will define the key project output variables to be tracked during the project. Identifying the types of defects to be tracked and determining a method for calculating overall throughput time is important. Next, the black belt and team will gather to collect and record the voice-of-customer needs and desires with respect to the process, which is done with quality function deployment and other tools related to voice of the customer. In addition, identifying the desired values for 30,000-foot-level metrics is necessary. After doing this, the Six Sigma team and black belt will benchmark similar processes and create a flowchart that represents the process needs. The next step will be to consider applying lean tools such as the logic flow map, time-value diagram, and spaghetti chart. If necessary, the process can be tweaked at this point.

After applying lean tools and making any necessary adjustments to the process plan, the process DFSS project team will create a project management plan for actually creating the process. At this point the team should discuss the implications of modeling the process with a process modeling computer program. The next step will be to conduct a process failure modes and effects analysis. This analysis will indicate the appropriate changes for the process. Next, the black belt and team will create a list of all the variables likely to be key process input variables, or KPIVs. The process DFSS project team will then perform a DOE (design of experiments) that simulates the process. In addition, the process DFSS project team may want to apply pass/fail functional tests. If the tests indicate extreme values for key process input variables, then this information should be taken into consideration during the design of experiments.

The typical process DFSS project team first will conduct DOE and then will compose a DOE collective response capability assessment (DCRCA). As part of the DCRCA, the team will create a probability plot of the DOE responses and then compare them to the customer requirements relative to the process. The next step will be to use basic procedures for analyzing DOE should the desired percentage points from a probability plot fall outside the conformance levels. Next, the team must adjust the process design, which is done with the knowledge obtained from DOE. If done properly, the subsequent DOE should deliver the desired results. Next, the process DFSS project team will create a control plan related to the key process input variables

found to be statistically significant. The subsequent step is to finish the plan for monitoring key process output variables from the 30,000-foot level.

After finishing the plan for tracking key process output variables from the 30,000-foot level, the process DFSS project team typically will gather and organize the key process output variables as a function of key process input variables. This step is done in case closer investigation of causes is required in the future. Next, the team will update and abide by the project management plan for process creation. The process DFSS team then will run a pilot for the finished process. During this pilot run, key process output variables must be tracked at the 30,000-foot level. Next, the team must determine whether the desired levels of the process have been met by the capability and performance. When desired levels are not met, a DMAIC strategy may be implemented for process improvement. Once the process has been brought to the desired level, the results of the project should be documented and passed around the organization. If the results of this project can be applied to other areas of the business, this should be the focus of future projects.

DFX

Design for X (DFX) is a blanket term for the set of strategies for improving the efficiency of product development processes. One of the key insights of DFX is that previous approaches to design have placed too much emphasis on the resulting product rather than on the process that led to it. In DFX, the design process is reviewed continuously and improved, and the resulting improvements in output speak for themselves. Various forms of DFX are appropriate for particular purposes: design for recyclability, design for ergonomics, design for quality, and design for test, to name a few. These systems have features in common, such as a tendency to simplicity and a reliance on fewer parts. When discrete units in an organization carry out design duties, each of these units may be operating according to a different DFX methodology, but the general trend of work will be the same for all.

Axiomatic design

In axiomatic design, the purpose of work is to respond to constraints. The design object is something desired by the customer, and the process of design is strictly observed. This process begins with the selection of design objectives that satisfy a defined set of customer attributes. The design team then creates a list of ideas that conceivably could fulfill customer requirements. The next step is to analyze these solution alternatives and determine which solution best meets the design objectives. The final step is to implement this design. Axiomatic design programs consist of four domains: customer, function, physical, and process. Besides creating quality products, the larger mission of axiomatic design is to encourage a continuous processing of information among these four domains.

Porter's five forces analysis

In 1979, Michael E. Porter of the Harvard Business School expounded his five forces analysis of business strategy. This strategy is a process for assessing a market before entering. A market is considered attractive if entry is likely to prove profitable. According to Porter, the five forces that influence the attractiveness of a market are the threat of new competition, the threat of substitute products, the bargaining power of customers, the bargaining power of suppliers, and the competitive rivalries within the industry. Porter describes these forces as the micro-environment of the business as opposed to the macro-environment of the whole economy and climate for business. Three of Porter's forces relate to horizontal competition, or competition from rival businesses, while two relate to vertical competition, or pressures applied by suppliers and customers.

Threat of new competition
The threat of new competition is one of the five forces outlined by Porter. An attractive market inevitably will receive new entrants. In some industries, however, blocking entrants is possible. For instance, patent agreements may limit participation. If a market is extremely susceptible to new competitors, the overall profits of all firms likely will be driven down in the long run. Eventually, all of the remaining firms will tend to achieve merely average profits. One factor that can influence the possibility of new entrants is brand equity, or the value a business earns simply by being in the market for a long time. For instance, a new cola would have to be very aggressive to steal market share from the current giants of this market. This necessity makes entry less appealing. New entrants also would be discouraged if customers are very loyal to the existing firms, or switching brands was expensive for customers.

Threat of substitute products or services
The threat of substitute products or services is one of the five forces outlined by Porter in his program for industry analysis. If customers easily can vary their purchasing habits or if the niche for one product can be superseded by another, then the market is less attractive. When substituting products or services is easy, demand will be tied closely to price. In other words, if the price goes up, customers will be more likely to choose a different product or service. To determine the threat of substitute products or services, a business should evaluate the

tendency of customers to substitute, the costs of switching purchasing patterns, and the general perception of differences between products or services. The business also should consider how easy it will be for customers to make the switch. Finally, the business may want to consider whether small differences in quality or prices are likely to encourage customers to choose substitute products or services.

Bargaining power of customers

The bargaining power of customers is one of the five forces outlined by Porter in his program for industry analysis. If customers are powerful, then the business will be less profitable. Powerful customers are very sensitive to changes in price, so firms cannot raise prices without expecting to see a strong decline in demand. A number of factors can affect the bargaining power of customers. First, when the concentration of buyers is large relative to the concentration of firms, customers will be more powerful. When customers depend on the existing channels of distribution, they will be less powerful. If customers can obtain information about products easily, they are more powerful. When the products in an industry are not very different, customers are more powerful because less disincentive exists for them to switch brands. Finally, if substitute products readily are available, customers will have more power.

Bargaining power of suppliers

The bargaining power of suppliers is one of the five forces outlined by Porter in his program for industry analysis. When suppliers have more bargaining power, less incentive exists for a business to enter the market. A number of factors influence the bargaining power of suppliers. When the supplier switching costs are large relative to the firm switching costs, less profit exists for a firm entering the market. On the other hand, when numerous substitute inputs exists, firms are better able to seize profits. When distribution channels are strong, firms have a better opportunity to establish profitable supply chains. When a great deal of competition exists among suppliers, the advantage goes to the manufacturer. Finally, when switching suppliers has little or no impact on cost or quality, then the bargaining power of suppliers is diminished significantly.

Intensity of competitive rivalry

The intensity of competitive rivalry is one of the five forces outlined by Porter in his program for industry analysis. This is typically the largest determinant of the level of competition in the industry. It depends on a number of factors. When businesses are able to maintain their competitive advantage through continuous innovation, the market will be less competitive. If advertising is expensive, then the market is less likely to be competitive, because there will be a prohibitive cost for firms to battle one another in the media. When one firm in an industry has a strong competitive strategy, there is less likely to be decent competition. Finally, an industry will be more competitive when there can be competition between online and offline companies.

Criticisms

Five forces analysis remains popular in business theory despite having some strong critics. One common criticism of five forces analysis is its assumption that profit only arises from the creation of structural advantages. In other words, five forces analysis assumes the only way to get ahead in an industry is by barring other firms from entering. This model also assumes is no cooperation (or even collusion) among buyers, competitors, and suppliers. Five forces analysis also assumes businesses' ability to obtain accurate and comprehensive information about the five forces. Some business theorists have evolved five forces analysis by allowing for some cooperation between competing firms. Other commentators have declared that the government should be treated as a sixth force because regulations and legislation have such profound impact on the advisability of entering a given market. Porter has rejected this last argument, saying that as originally written, the five forces imply government. One final criticism of five forces analysis is its focus exclusively on factors external to the firm. Finally, it does not consider the strengths and weaknesses of the business, itself.

TRIZ

One approach to DFSS is the theory of inventive problem-solving, often referred to by its Russian acronym TRIZ. This approach is useful when attempts to improve one element of production cause a deterioration of other elements. This occurrence is known as a technical or functional contradiction. TRIZ attempts to resolve a contradiction by transcending it rather than by making sacrifices on either side. In the TRIZ methodology, some problems have known solutions, and some problems have unknown solutions. The solutions to problems are classified further by the level of expertise required to find and implement them. A standard solution requires basic knowledge, while a solution within the same paradigm represents an improvement of the existing system. Some solutions necessitate an advancement of the contemporary scientific understanding of the problem; obviously, these problems will prove the most difficult to solve. A problem with no known solution is referred to in TRIZ as an inventive problem.

Eight laws of system development
The theory of inventive problem-solving, or TRIZ, was largely the work of a Russian mechanical engineer named Genrich Altshuller. Altshuller developed eight basic laws for system development, which he claimed could be applied anywhere, although they were based on engineering systems. The laws are as follows:

- Law of system completeness: a system is the synthesis of disparate parts.
- Law of increasing ideality: functions tend to get less complex and more productive.
- Law of harmonization: energy is transferred with increasing efficiency.
- Law of energy transfer in the system: many inventive problems are based on the flow of energy.
- Law of uneven development of parts: different aspects of the system will develop at different rates, and the overall success of the system will be limited by the least-developed aspect.
- Law of transition from macro to micro: solutions will decrease in physical size.
- Law of increasing substance-field involvement: systems will be viewed as two substances interacting through a field.
- Law of transition to a super system: each solution system will become part of a greater system.

Application
In the theory of inventive problem-solving, otherwise known as TRIZ, the best solutions resolve a technical or functional contradiction without requiring sacrifice on either side. In other words, improvement of one aspect of a system should not cause deterioration of another aspect of a system. One way to encourage this process is to look outside of the field in which the problem lies. According to Genrich Altshuller, the primary creator of TRIZ, engineers should look for solutions in other areas of research. He proposed that only forty

categories of solution exist; furthermore, by looking in turn at each type of solution, an engineer could come across novel ways of resolving technical or functional contradictions. Essentially, TRIZ offers a list of options for problem-solvers. Problems are made abstract so affinities with problems in other fields may be discovered. One happy consequence of TRIZ is that problems and solutions are increasingly categorized in generic terms, making them easier to find for researchers.

Eight Disciplines problem-solving method

The Eight Disciplines problem-solving method identifies and solves recurring problems. This method features eight stages, or disciplines, as well as a preliminary planning stage (D0). The first discipline (D1) is to create a team of experts. The second discipline (D2) is to define the problem and enumerate its features. The third discipline (D3) is to create and implement a short-term plan for containing the problem. The fourth discipline (D4) is to pinpoint the root causes and escape points of the problem. Escape points are the reasons the problem has not yet been identified. The fifth discipline (D5) is to select and confirm a permanent set of solutions. The sixth discipline (D6) is to implement and evaluate the solutions. The seventh discipline (D7) is to take action to prevent the problem from occurring again. The eighth and final discipline (D8) is to celebrate and express gratitude to the team.

RPR method of problem-solving

The rapid problem resolution (RPR) method of problem-solving particularly is good at identifying and resolving nagging and recurrent problems. The RPR method has two components: the core process and the supporting techniques. The core process consists of three phases: discovery, investigation, and resolution. In the discovery phase, the team must collect and review information and then agree on the meaning of the information. In the investigation phase, the team must create a plan to collect information about the problem and then use the information gathered to identify the root cause of the problem. In the resolution or fix stage, the team takes their learning from the second stage and uses it to create and implement a permanent solution. This solution must be monitored. The second component of the RPR method, supporting techniques, is a set of tools for accomplishing the core process.

Practice Test

Practice Questions

1. Which key performance indicator is calculated by subtracting current costs from ideal costs?
    a. Cost of poor quality
    b. Revenue growth
    c. Competitive quality
    d. Performance on quality improvement

2. Which type of chart is appropriate when sample size is variable and each sample may contain more than one instance of the targeted condition?
    a. P chart
    b. Autocorrelation chart
    c. U chart
    d. X-bar chart

3. What is the purpose of PERT analysis during the analyze phase of DMAIC?
    a. To identify the most influential steps in a process
    b. To monitor improvements in cycle time
    c. To identify the critical path of a process
    d. To reduce cycle time

4. Which of the following is a disadvantage of using engineering process control devices to prevent deviation?
    a. The devices must be monitored by human operators.
    b. The use of these devices precludes the use of statistical process controls.
    c. These devices require constant maintenance.
    d. These devices cannot handle multiple inputs.

5. Which form of leveling typically includes the use of heijunka boxes?
    a. Leveling by volume
    b. Leveling by product
    c. Demand leveling
    d. Customer leveling

6. Which parameter of a statistical distribution relates to the sharpness of its peak?
    a. Central tendency
    b. Kurtosis
    c. Skewness
    d. Standard deviation

7. If a mixed-level experimental design has four factors with three levels and two factors with three levels, how many total runs are required for the experiment?
 a. 18
 b. 24
 c. 64
 d. 72

8. Which method of creating a prioritization matrix is appropriate when time is limited?
 a. Partial analytical method
 b. Consensus–criteria method
 c. Full analytical method
 d. Summary method

9. In which design is it possible to have two-factor interactions confounded with one another as well as with higher-order interactions?
 a. Resolution IV
 b. Resolution V
 c. Resolution VI
 d. Resolution VII

10. Which of the following is a disadvantage of higher-order multiple regression models?
 a. These models do a poor job of defining the area around a stationary point.
 b. Comprehensive and detailed experiments must be performed on the main effects.
 c. These models rarely have clear peaks and valleys.
 d. Small regions are difficult to perceive.

11. In response surface analysis, which of the following values for s and t weights would indicate that the upper and lower boundaries are more important than the target?
 a. –0.3
 b. 0
 c. 1
 d. 7

12. Which type of human error is typically limited to a particular task?
 a. Willful
 b. Inadvertent
 c. Technique
 d. Selective

13. If a process consists of two tasks, the first of which has a 0.04 probability of error and the second of which has a 0.03 probability of error, and these errors can occur at the same time, what is the overall likelihood of an error occurring during the process?
 a. 0.0012
 b. 0.0688
 c. 0.0120
 d. 0.1688

14. In a histogram, the number of bars is equal to
    a. the square root of the total number of data values.
    b. the square root of the range of data.
    c. the range of data divided by the total number of data values.
    d. the number of data observations.

15. Which of the following diagrams indicates the critical path of a process?
    a. Gantt chart
    b. Work breakdown structure
    c. Value stream analysis
    d. Matrix diagram

16. During which stage of DMAIC is level loading typically performed?
    a. Define
    b. Control
    c. Improve
    d. Measure

17. Which of the following increases the power of an estimation of the confidence interval on the mean?
    a. A sample population with a normal distribution
    b. A smaller number of samples
    c. A known standard deviation
    d. An unknown standard deviation

18. Which of Altshuller's eight laws for system development asserts that functions will tend toward simplicity and efficiency?
    a. Law of transition to a super system
    b. Law of increasing substance-field involvement
    c. Law of increasing ideality
    d. Law of harmonization

19. In an analysis of variance, how is the F statistic used?
    a. To compare the mean square treatment with the mean square error
    b. To estimate the process average
    c. To find the variation within each subgroup
    d. To find the variation between different subgroups

20. In a numerical matrix diagram using a ten-point scale, which of the following values would indicate the strongest relationship?
    a. 9
    b. 1/10
    c. 1
    d. –1/5

21. If there are 32 observations in an experiment, it is typical to run autocorrelations from lag 1 to
    a. lag 4.
    b. lag 8.
    c. lag 16.
    d. lag 32.

22. Which of the following is a disadvantage of using enumerative statistics?
    a. It is difficult to determine whether the samples are representative.
    b. These statistics do not produce an assumed distribution.
    c. They cannot be applied to process baseline estimation.
    d. Values are drawn from a static population.

23. Which distribution is appropriate for a continuous set of data with a fixed lower boundary but no upper boundary?
    a. Johnson
    b. Exponential
    c. Normal
    d. Lognormal

24. In metrology, what is the degree to which a measurement can be compared to a known standard with confidence called?
    a. Traceability
    b. Measurement uncertainty
    c. Calibration
    d. Engineering tolerance

25. Which of the following autocorrelation functions would indicate the strongest correlation?
    a. 0.1
    b. −0.8
    c. 0.9
    d. −0.2

26. In Porter's five forces analysis, what is the likely result of strong distribution channels?
    a. Switching distributers will have no impact on cost.
    b. There will be more incentive for new firms to enter the market.
    c. Suppliers will have less bargaining power.
    d. Firms will have a hard time maintaining competitive advantage.

27. In most cases, what is the lowest coefficient of determination that is considered acceptable in a linearity analysis?
    a. 10%
    b. 30%
    c. 50%
    d. 70%

28. Which type of Pareto chart would be the least useful?
    a. One in which the bars represent costs
    b. One in which the cumulative percentage line is steep
    c. One in which all the bars are roughly the same height
    d. One in which the bars on the left are significantly taller than the bars on the right

29. Which median test is the most appropriate for handling outliers?
    a. Mood's median test
    b. Kruskal–Wallis test
    c. Mann–Whitney test
    d. Kolmogorov–Smirnov test

30. Which distribution should be used when the targeted characteristic may appear more than once per unit?
    a. Binomial
    b. Exponential
    c. Lognormal
    d. Poisson

31. What is the final step in a kaizen event?
    a. Modifying the solution after implementation
    b. Celebrating success
    c. Implementing a solution
    d. Laying off employees

32. If all of the data points on an Np chart fall between the upper and lower control limits, the process is
    a. representative.
    b. stable.
    c. efficient.
    d. erratic.

33. What is the Japanese term for *inconsistency*?
    a. Mura
    b. Muki
    c. Muda
    d. Muri

34. In nominal group technique, how many pieces of paper should each participant receive if there are 40 options to be considered?
    a. 2
    b. 4
    c. 6
    d. 8

35. What is the term for the degree to which an experimental design allows all the indicated parameters to be measured independently of one another?
    a. Autonomy
    b. Normalization
    c. Orthogonality
    d. Balance

36. Which of the following factors is not included in the calculation of risk priority number?
    a. Detection level
    b. Severity
    c. Expense
    d. Likelihood

37. In an exponentially weighted moving-average chart, which of the following weighting factors would be best for detecting small shifts?
    a. 0.4
    b. 0.19
    c. 0.38
    d. 0.47

38. How many runs would be required in a complete factorial design if there are four levels and three factors?
    a. 7
    b. 12
    c. 64
    d. 81

39. In which of these scenarios would batching be appropriate?
    a. Setup time for the activity is significant.
    b. The process contains multiple steps.
    c. Completed products must be shipped in bulk.
    d. Employees must wait for a certain amount of materials before beginning a task.

40. Which of the following run tests identifies shifts in the process mean?
    a. Run test 4
    b. Run test 6
    c. Run test 7
    d. Run test 8

41. Which of the following items is NOT a part of the typical tollgate review?
    a. Milestone list
    b. Project deliverables document
    c. Check sheet
    d. Gantt chart

42. In kaizen, what is the term that refers to the idea that one step in a process should be completed only when the subsequent steps are ready?
   a. Flow
   b. Poka-yoke
   c. Pull
   d. Perfection

43. Which business performance measure is calculated by subtracting current cash outflows from current cash inflows?
   a. Revenue growth
   b. Net present value
   c. Return on investment
   d. Margin

44. Which of the following is NOT one of the phases of rapid problem resolution?
   a. Resolution
   b. Investigation
   c. Discovery
   d. Implementation

45. Which pioneer of quality control wrote *Quality Is Free*?
   a. W. Edward Deming
   b. Joseph M. Juran
   c. Armand V. Feigenbaum
   d. Philip B. Crosby

46. Which experimental design is similar to a central composite design but without corner or extreme points?
   a. John's ¾ design
   b. Plackett–Burman design
   c. Box–Behnken design
   d. Mixed–level design

47. Which of the following is NOT one of the seven classic wastes?
   a. Motion
   b. Transportation
   c. Inventory
   d. Indecision

48. In order to calibrate an instrument, one must know the _____ of both the instrument and the standard.
   a. durability
   b. traceability
   c. tolerance
   d. measurement uncertainty

49. Which of the following is an advantage of the transformation technique known as *normalization*?
    a. Normalization screens irrelevant factors from a nonlinear experimental design.
    b. Normalization balances the experimental array.
    c. Normalization places all values on a common scale from 0 to 2.
    d. Normalization is more effective in nonlinear experiments.

50. In a Kano model, what value is always on the *y*-axis?
    a. Time
    b. Satisfaction
    c. Quality
    d. Price

Answers and Explanations

1. A: The *cost of poor quality* is calculated by subtracting current costs from ideal costs. This is just a rough estimate as the exact value of the cost of poor quality is unknowable. The point of estimating the cost of poor quality is to get a general idea of what savings could be made available through remediation and improvement efforts. *Revenue growth* is calculated by determining the net increase in sales figures over a particular interval. *Competitive quality* is an umbrella term for a set of metrics related to the parts of performance that have the most influence on sales. Some competitive quality measures depend on obtaining information from customers. *Performance on quality improvement,* finally, is a subjective metric that includes the number of completed and active projects, the financial results of these projects, and the number of employees and hours required for the project.

2. C: A *U chart* is appropriate when sample size is variable and each sample may contain more than one instance of the targeted condition. These are control charts most appropriate for handling attributes data. A *P chart,* on the other hand, is better for measuring the percentage of samples with a particular characteristic when sample size is variable and the characteristic will either be present or absent. An *autocorrelation chart* indicates the relationships between various factors in the process. An *X-bar chart,* finally, is a control chart for variables data, in which the subgroup averages are assessed to determine the process location variation over time.

3. C: The purpose of program evaluation and review techniques (PERT) analysis during the analyze phase of DMAIC is to identify the critical path of a process. PERT analysis uses activity network diagrams and other charts to isolate the tasks on the critical path. Note that the critical path is the sequence of necessarily consecutive steps in a task, such that the sum of the durations required for each step on the critical path will be the minimum amount of time required for the total process. PERT analysis may also be used to identify the most influential steps in a process, though this takes place during the define stage of DMAIC: Likewise, PERT analysis may be used during the improve stage to monitor adjustments to cycle time. The overarching goal of PERT analysis is to reduce cycle time, but this answer choice is too general to be correct.

4. B: One disadvantage of using engineering process controls to prevent deviation is that the use of these devices precludes the use of statistical process controls. An *engineering process control* is a mechanism that automatically adjusts inputs when it detects variations in the process. A thermostat is a basic example of an engineering process control. It is not necessary for these devices to be monitored by human operators, and in most cases, engineering process controls do not require constant maintenance. The constant adjustments made by these devices, however, mean that any data related to their activities is not independent and, therefore, cannot be analyzed with statistical process control charts. However, the engineering process controls used by heavy industry are capable of handling a number of different inputs and outputs simultaneously.

5. B: Leveling by product typically includes the use of heijunka boxes. A *heijunka box* is a tool for scheduling in which the tasks to be completed and the estimated times for initiation and completion are listed. The point of leveling by product is to reduce inefficiency by adjusting the mix of products or the order in which they are produced. Leveling by volume, by contrast, is an approach to reducing inefficiency in which production is aligned with

- 115 -

average demand. Demand leveling is a series of strategies that attempt to make customer demand more uniform and predictable. There is no such thing as customer leveling.

6. B: *Kurtosis* is the parameter of a statistical distribution related to the sharpness of the peak. In a normal distribution, where the points resemble the standard bell curve, the kurtosis value is one. If the peak is sharper, the kurtosis value will be higher than one; if the peak is less severe, the kurtosis value will be less than one. *Central tendency* is the general trend of the data: In an asymmetrical distribution, the median is roughly equivalent to the central tendency, while in an asymmetrical distribution, the mean is a better marker. *Skewness* is basically the difference between the mean and the mode of a data set. The *mode* of the data set is the value that appears most often. Finally, the *standard deviation* of the data set is the average amount of variation from the mean.

7. D: If a mixed-level experimental design has four factors with three levels and two factors with three levels, 72 total runs will be required. The formula for calculating the number of required runs for a mixed-level experimental design is similar to that used on a complete factorial design. The number of factors must be raised to the power equal to the number of levels for that factor. So, for this problem, the total number of runs is calculated as $4^3 + 2^3 = 64 + 8 = 72$.

8. B: When time is limited, the consensus–criteria method should be used to create a prioritization matrix. In this method, a group of people are each allotted 100 points, which they then allocate across a series of criteria according to perceived importance. Prioritization matrices are used to identify those projects that will create the most value improvement over the long term. Also, organizations use participation matrices to identify the projects that will contribute the most to the achievement of the organizational goals. Besides the consensus–criteria method, the other method for creating a prioritization matrix is called the *full analytical method*. In this method, all of the various options are listed, and the members of the team assign a numerical value to each.

9. A: In a resolution IV experimental design, it is possible to have two-factor interactions confounded with one another as well as with higher-order interactions. The point of design resolution is to determine the types of interactions that may be estimated independently within a particular design. When factors and interactions are confounded, they may not be estimated. Resolution V designs feature main-factor and two-factor interactions that are not confounded with one another, though it is possible that these interactions may be confounded with higher-order interactions. In a resolution VI experimental design, main-factor and two-factor interactions are not confounded with one another or with three-factor interactions, but three-factor and higher-order interactions may be confounded with one another. In a resolution VII design, main-factor, two-factor, and three-factor interactions are not confounded with one another, but each of these interactions may be confounded with higher-order interactions. It is also possible for four-factor and higher-order interactions in a resolution VII design to be confounded.

10. B: One disadvantage of higher-order multiple regression models is that comprehensive and detailed experiments must be performed on the main effects. Otherwise, it will not be wise to assume that the results of the higher-order multiple regression models are useful or accurate. However, higher-order multiple regression models have a number of advantages. For one thing, they are excellent at clearly defining the area around a stationary point. They typically have well-defined peaks and valleys, which enable analysis. Also, they are very

effective at mapping small regions in the process, so they are able to achieve a high level of precision and detail.

11. D: In response surface analysis, values of 7 for the s and t weights would indicate that the upper and lower boundaries are more important than the target. In phase 2 of response surface analysis, the s and t weights are based on the relationship between the target and the boundary. When the target and the boundary have equal value, the s and t weights are 1. When the target is more important than the boundary, the s and t weights are between 1 and 10. When the boundary is more important than the target, the s and t weights are between 0.1 and 1.

12. C: Technique error is typically limited to a particular task. Six Sigma experts identify three categories of human error: technique, inadvertent, and willful. Technique errors are the result of a lack of comprehension or poor training. It is more likely that technique errors will occur on difficult tasks. Inadvertent errors are slightly different because they occur by accident even when an employee is experienced and understands the task. It is impossible to entirely eliminate inadvertent errors so long as there are human operators. A willful error is made intentionally by an employee. The best way to reduce willful errors is to maintain high morale and incentivize high performance.

13. B: If a process consists of two tasks, the first of which has a 0.04 probability of error and the second of which has a 0.03 probability of error, and these errors can occur at the same time, the overall likelihood of an error occurring during the process is 0.0688. The formula for the probability of two events that can happen at the same time is $P(A \cup B) = P(A) + P(B) - P(A \cap B)$, meaning the probability of A or B occurring is equal to the probability of A plus the probability of B minus the probability of A and B. In this case, then, the probability would be calculated as $0.04 + 0.03 - (0.04 \times 0.03) = 0.0688$.

14. A: In a histogram, the number of bars is equal to the square root of the total number of data values. Histograms look like bar graphs, but the bars on a histogram represent the number of observations that fall within a particular range. Histograms are often used to locate multiple distributions or apply a distribution to capability analysis. The width of each bar in a histogram is calculated by dividing the range of data by the number of bars. The range of data is determined by subtracting the minimum data value from the maximum data value. On a histogram, the x-axis represents the data values of each bar, and the y-axis indicates the number of observations.

15. A: A *Gantt chart* indicates the critical path of a process. The *critical path* is the sequence of steps that have a direct bearing on the overall length of the process. Some steps can be delayed without elongating the overall duration of the process: These steps are not considered to be on the critical path. A *work breakdown structure* depicts the organization of a process. To create a work breakdown structure, one isolates the various components of a problem and then considers the various contingencies associated with each component. A *value stream analysis* determines the elements of a process that add value to the finished product. These elements are targeted for special attention. Finally, a *matrix diagram* depicts the relative strengths of the relationships between the items in different groups. A matrix diagram might indicate causal relationships between various factors in a process or might simply indicate which of the factors are related.

16. C: Level loading is typically performed during the improve stage of DMAIC. The intention of level loading is to make the flow of orders in a process more regular and predictable. When level loading is effective, fewer inventory checks and less wait time should be required during the course of a process. Level loading depends on careful measurement of takt time earlier in the DMAIC process.

17. C: A known standard deviation increases the power of an estimation of the confidence interval on the mean. Indeed, when the standard deviation is known, the z tables may be used to find the confidence interval on the mean; when the standard deviation is unknown, the t tables must be used. The confidence interval on the mean is the percentage of samples that will contain the true population mean. It is assumed that the sample population will follow a normal distribution. When there are more samples, this increases the power of the estimation of the confidence interval on the mean.

18. C: Altshuller's law of increasing ideality asserts that functions will tend toward simplicity and efficiency. Genrich Altshuller is famous for devising eight basic laws of system development, which form the philosophical core of his theory of inventive problem solving (TRIZ). These laws were created to solve engineering problems, though Altshuller contended that they could be applied in any situation. The *law of increasing ideality* is essentially an optimistic vision of the evolution of functions over time. The *law of transition to a super system* asserts that the individual solutions created for specific systems will eventually become components of a larger, comprehensive system. The *law of increasing substance-field involvement* asserts that engineers will treat design problems as two individual materials interacting through a field, and the results of these interactions will be system improvements. *The law of harmonization* suggests that, as a system improves, energy will be transferred throughout it more efficiently.

19. A: In an analysis of variance, the *F statistic* is used to compare the mean square treatment with the mean square error. The *mean square treatment* is the average variation between the subsets, while the *mean square error* is the sum of the squares of the residuals. In order to trust the results of the F statistic, one must assume that the subsets have a normal distribution and unequal variance. The variation within each subgroup is calculated by taking repeated samples from the subgroup. The variation between different subgroups is found by comparing the averages of each subgroup.

20. B: In a numerical matrix diagram, a value of 1/10 would indicate the strongest relationship. Numerical matrix diagrams assign relationships values on a scale to indicate the strength of the interactions between variables. This diagram indicates the direction of the relationship by expressing the value as either a whole number or a fraction: That is, on a 10-point scale, a 10 would indicate the strongest possible relationship in one direction and 1/10 would indicate the strongest possible relationship in the other. Therefore, a value of 1/10 would indicate a stronger relationship than a value of 9. Negative values do not appear on a numerical matrix diagram.

21. B: If there are 32 observations in an experiment, it is typical to run autocorrelations from lag 1 to lag 8. The basic calculation for the number of autocorrelations in an experiment is lag 1 to lag $x/4$, in which x is the number of observations. Because there are 32 observations in this experiment, autocorrelations should run from lag 1 to lag 8. The lag is the difference between correlated observations. In lag 1, for instance, observation 1 is correlated with observation 2, observation 2 is correlated with observation 3, observation 3

is correlated with observation 4, and so on. In lag 8, observation 1 would be correlated with observation 9, observation 2 with observation 10, observation 3 with observation 11, and so on. An experiment with 32 observations would include all of the intervening correlations between lag 1 and lag 8 (i.e., lags 2 through 7).

22. D: One disadvantage of using enumerative statistics is that values are drawn from a static population. If a dynamic process is to be measured, as is often the case in Six Sigma, it is necessary to use analytical statistics. The other answer choices allude to advantages of enumerative statistics. For instance, one advantage of enumerative statistics is that they make it easy to determine whether samples are representative. A representative sample is one extracted from the population without any bias. Enumerative statistics provide an assumed distribution as well as a confidence level and a set of confidence intervals. Finally, enumerative statistics may be applied to process baseline estimation, namely for the purpose of assessing random samples.

23. D: A *lognormal distribution* is appropriate for a continuous set of data with a fixed lower boundary but no upper boundary. In most cases, the lower boundary on a lognormal distribution is zero. These distributions can be tested with a goodness-of-fit test. A *Johnson distribution* is more appropriate for continuous data that, for whatever reason, is inappropriate for a normal or exponential distribution. An *exponential distribution* is appropriate for any set of continuous data, though these distributions are most often used for frequency data. A *normal distribution* is appropriate for a set of continuous data with neither an upper nor a lower boundary. The normal distribution follows the pattern of the classic bell curve.

24. A: In metrology, the degree to which a measurement can be compared to a known standard with confidence is called *traceability*. Experts on measurement are aware that every gauge is to some extent inaccurate (i.e., it contains measurement uncertainty), but it is important that these inaccuracies themselves be measurable. Six Sigma projects require a number of different measurements taken at different times and in different conditions, and it is essential that these measurements have essentially the same level of traceability.

25. C: An autocorrelation function of 0.9 would indicate the strongest correlation. The range of autocorrelation functions and partial autocorrelation functions extends from –1 to 1. The strength of the correlation is indicated by the distance from 0 (i.e., the absolute value) regardless of whether the value is on the positive or negative side. Therefore, an autocorrelation function of 0.9 would indicate a stronger correlation than would functions of 0.1, –0.8, and –0.2.

26. C: In Porter's five forces analysis, the likely result of strong distribution channels is that suppliers will have less bargaining power. This is because firms that feel confident in their supply chains will be less likely to accept disadvantageous terms from their vendors. Five forces analysis was developed by Michael E. Porter as a tool for assessing the potential for success in a given market. The five forces are the likelihood of new competition, the threat of substitute products, the bargaining power of customers, the bargaining power of suppliers, and the level of competition within the industry. The existence of strong distribution channels would indicate that switching distributers would have an impact on cost and that new firms would be discouraged from entering the market. Also, strong distribution channels would tend to reinforce competitive advantage.

27. D: In most cases, the lowest coefficient of determination that is considered acceptable in a linearity analysis is 70%. The coefficient of determination indicates the adequacy of the measurement system. A *linearity analysis* is a study of the potential for bias error for a particular measurement system at different points in the equipment's operating range. It is important that the Six Sigma team know that the measurement system will be roughly as accurate at all points during a process.

28. C: The least useful type of Pareto chart would be one in which all the bars are roughly the same height. A *Pareto chart* is used to identify the most important and urgent problems in a process. It is based on the *Pareto principle,* which is the idea that a process can be improved dramatically through attention to the few most important problems. It is essential that the bars on a Pareto chart represent tangible values, like cost or count. A Pareto chart will not be useful if it is based on percentages or rates. The most useful Pareto charts have several large bars on the left, indicating problems that are significantly more important than others. Similarly, a steeply ascending line on a Pareto chart indicates that a few of the identified factors are very important and, therefore, that the chart will be useful. If all of the bars on a Pareto chart are roughly the same height, no one factor is more important than another, and therefore, it will be impossible to generate an unusual amount of benefit by solving a single problem.

29. A: Of the given tests, the Mood's median test would be the most appropriate for handling outliers. A *Mood's median test* is a method of nonparametric estimation similar to a chi-square test. This form of test is better at handling outliers, but the *Kruskal–Wallis* does a better job of evaluating certain distributions. In both the Mood's median and Kruskal–Wallis tests, the null hypothesis is that all population medians are equal, while the alternative hypothesis is that not all of the medians are equal. The *Mann–Whitney test* is closer to the Kruskal–Wallis. The *Kolmogorov–Smirnov* is a goodness-of-fit test that provides more specific results than a chi-square test.

30. D: A *Poisson distribution* should be used when the targeted characteristic may appear more than once per unit. In order for a Poisson distribution to be effective, the data should consist of positive whole numbers, and the experimental trials should be independent. A *binomial distribution* is appropriate for situations in which the units in the population will only have one of two possible characteristics (e.g., off or on). An *exponential distribution* is appropriate for measurement data, especially frequency. A *lognormal distribution* is appropriate for continuous data with a fixed lower boundary but no upper boundary. In most cases, the lower boundary of a lognormal distribution is zero.

31. B: The final step in a kaizen event is celebrating success. Kaizen experts insist that this is an important part of the process because it builds organizational morale and establishes proper conditions for success on similar projects in the future. In general, the steps in a kaizen event are providing employees with basic training, defining the problem, measuring performance, brainstorming, deciding upon a solution, implementing the solution, making adjustments, gathering results, and celebrating.

32. B: If all of the data points on an *Np* chart fall between the upper and lower control limits, the process is stable. So long as all of the variation is within these limits, it can be assumed to be the result of common causes. Assuming the chart is reliable, data points that fall outside the upper and lower control limits are the result of special-cause variation. At the least, the presence of data points outside the upper and lower control limits identifies areas

where employees will need to conduct further research. *Np* charts are control charts for analyzing attributes data. These charts are used when the sample size is regular and the targeted condition may only occur once per sample.

33. A: The Japanese term for inconsistency is *mura*. Eliminating *mura* often requires a comprehensive redesign of the process, for which reason many Six Sigma programs have focused instead on reducing *muda*, which is wasteful or unproductive activity. *Muri*, or overloading, is the third form of waste identified by the Toyota Production System. *Muki* is not a term in quality management.

34. D: In nominal group technique, each participant should receive eight pieces of paper if there are 40 options to be considered. Each participant will then write one of the options down on each piece of paper, along with its rank (first through eighth). It is typical for each participant to receive eight pieces of paper when there are more than 35 options. When there are from 20 to 35 options, the typical number of papers for each person is six. When there are fewer than 20 options to be considered, it is typical for each member of the group to receive four pieces of paper. Once all of the group members turn their rankings in, the various options are compared, and the most popular are given further consideration.

35. C: The term for the degree to which an experimental design allows all the indicated parameters to be measured independently of one another is *orthogonality*. This is an essential characteristic of experimental design. Balance, on the other hand, is not necessary. An experiment may have either *design balance,* when the design array has columns with equal numbers of levels for each parameter, or *data balance,* when each data point has roughly the same influence on parameter definition. *Autonomy* is not a characteristic of experimental design. *Normalization* is a technique of transformation in which data values are placed on a common range for easier comparison.

36. C: Expense is not one of the factors included in the calculation of risk priority number. Risk priority number is calculated by multiplying severity, likelihood, and detection level. The severity of the risk is the significance of its occurrence. Various industries have created standardized tables for indicating the severity of common risks. The likelihood of a risk is simply the chances of it happening. Finally, the detection level is based on the number of modes for identifying the error or failure as well as the chances that any one of these modes will be successful in detection. A common formula for calculating risk priority number is to place all of these categories on a scale from 1 to 10 and then multiply them together. In this scenario, the maximum risk priority number would be 1,000.

37. B: In an exponentially weighted moving-average chart, a weighting factor of 0.19 would be best for detecting small shifts. Generally, a weighting factor around 0.2 is most appropriate for detecting small shifts. Larger shifts may be most effectively detected with a weighting factor of between 0.2 and 0.4. Exponentially weighted moving-average charts establish a weighting factor so that values can receive different emphases depending on their ages.

38. C: If there are four levels and three factors in a complete factorial design, 64 runs would be required. The number of required runs is calculated by raising the number of levels to a power equal to the number of factors. In this case, then, the calculation is performed as $4^3 = 64$. If the complete factorial design had five levels and three factors, the number of runs would be calculated as $5^3 = 125$.

39. A: Batching would be appropriate in a scenario where setup time is significant. It was long thought that batching was a foolproof way to improve efficiency, but Six Sigma research indicated that batching strategies often lead to an increase in wait time and overall cycle time. One of the only situations in which batching would be appropriate would be when the preparation time for the activity is significant because there would then be a disincentive to set up and break down the equipment frequently.

40. B: Run test 6 identifies shifts in the process mean. The other run tests provide information about sampling errors. Run tests 1, 2, 3, and 5 also identify shifts in the process mean. Run tests are typically used in statistical process control programs to identify errors in data collection. Unfortunately, run tests are only able to identify the presence of errors and are not very good at pinpointing their locations.

41. D: A Gantt chart is not a part of the typical tollgate review. A *tollgate review* is a gathering of all the participants in a Six Sigma project, during which an assessment of the overall success of the project is made. Specifically, the participants in a tollgate review will identify whether the planning objectives have been met. In order to make this judgment, they may use basic check sheets, milestone lists, or project deliverables documents. However, a *Gantt chart*, which is used to identify the critical path of a project, is used exclusively during the define stage of DMAIC and is more aimed at improving efficiency then measuring the success of improvement efforts.

42. C: In kaizen, the idea that one step in a process should be completed only when the subsequent steps are ready is referred to as *pull*. This is opposite to the typical arrangement in manufacturing processes, in which materials are pushed through the process chain as they are completed. Kaizen recommends instead that materials be drawn along by vacuums created in the production chain. A process chain in which this occurs is said to have pull. *Flow*, meanwhile, is the continuous completion of a process. Organizations that adopt the kaizen philosophy attempt to make flow constant in every department and stage of processes. *Poka-yoke* is a Japanese system for error proofing, based on the premise that avoiding errors in the first run is worth a slightly higher cost. *Perfection* is the kaizen ideal of continuous improvement. Perfection is a goal that can never be attained but should be strived toward regardless.

43. B: *Net present value* is calculated by subtracting current cash outflows from current cash inflows. Net present value is an important variable when considering whether to make a particular investment. *Revenue growth,* meanwhile, is the change in sales figures over a particular interval. *Return on investment* is the amount of money received back by the company after an initial outlay of funds. Measuring return on investment is an effective way to determine whether an improvement or investment program has been worthwhile. *Margin,* finally, is the amount of funds a business must create in order to maintain its operations.

44. D: Implementation is not one of the phases of rapid problem resolution (RPR). RPR is an effective method for solving recurrent problems. The core process of RPR has three phases: discovery, investigation, and resolution. In the discovery phase, the team gathers information. In the investigation phase, the root cause of the problem is isolated. In the resolution phase, an appropriate solution is applied.

45. D: Philip B. Crosby wrote *Quality Is Free*, a book that revolutionized quality management by placing an explicit emphasis on getting processes right the first time. Crosby insisted that businesses are better served by investing more money in quality control on the first run and, thereby, avoiding the costs of defective products. W. Edwards Deming is famous for enumerating the seven deadly diseases of the workplace and 14 points of emphasis for management. Joseph M. Juran stressed the importance of customer satisfaction as a goal of quality control. Armand V. Feigenbaum is known for emphasizing four key actions in the implementation of quality management: establishing standards, creating metrics for conformance to these standards, resolving issues that impede conformance, and planning for continuous improvement.

46. C: A *Box–Behnken design* is similar to a central composite design but without corner or extreme points. For this reason, the Box–Behnken design can fully cover the experimental space without requiring as many points as a complete factorial design. Extreme factor-level combinations are not required for this design. A *Plackett–Burman design* is often used in lieu of a fractional factorial design when the number of runs in the experiment is equal to a factor of four. The *John's ¾ design* is so called because it only requires three-quarters of the runs of the typical fractional factorial design. This design is most often used when running a fractional factorial design indicates the need for further exploration of a limited set of interactions. A *mixed-level design* is used when factors have different numbers of levels.

47. D: Indecision is not one of the seven classic wastes. In the Japanese waste reduction system of *muda*, seven classic wastes are identified. These are transportation, inventory, motion, waiting, overprocessing, overproduction, and defects. The Toyota Production System emphasizes reducing each of these seven sources of waste as a means to improving efficiency.

48. D: In order to calibrate an instrument, one must know the *measurement uncertainty* of both the instrument and the standard. In most instances of calibration, the standard can have a maximum of 25% of the measurement uncertainty of the instrument. When this is the case, variations in standard will not significantly affect calibration. *Traceability* is a similar concept to measurement uncertainty, but it is the degree to which an instrument can be compared to a known standard, meaning that the standard itself will not have a defined traceability. In measurement, *tolerance* is the extent to which a measurement instrument will maintain its capability over a long duration. This is similar to the *durability* of the measurement instrument and standard.

49. A: One advantage of normalization is that it screens irrelevant factors from a nonlinear experimental design. However, normalization is more often used for linear experimental models. The process of normalization does not balance the experimental array; rather, the experimental array must be balanced in order for normalization to be a success. Normalization does place all the values on a common scale, but the scale ranges from –1 to 1. Finally, as indicated above, normalization may be used in nonlinear experiments, but it is typically more effective for linear experimental models.

50. B: In a Kano model, satisfaction is always on the *y*-axis and quality is always on the *x*-axis. In other words, increases in quality are tied to increases in satisfaction. One of the insights of the Kano model is that customer expectations and needs are always shifting and that, in order to maintain a constant level of satisfaction, a business needs to continuously improve processes and products.

Secret Key #1 - Time is Your Greatest Enemy

Pace Yourself

Wear a watch. At the beginning of the test, check the time (or start a chronometer on your watch to count the minutes), and check the time after every few questions to make sure you are "on schedule."

If you are forced to speed up, do it efficiently. Usually one or more answer choices can be eliminated without too much difficulty. Above all, don't panic. Don't speed up and just begin guessing at random choices. By pacing yourself, and continually monitoring your progress against your watch, you will always know exactly how far ahead or behind you are with your available time. If you find that you are one minute behind on the test, don't skip one question without spending any time on it, just to catch back up. Take 15 fewer seconds on the next four questions, and after four questions you'll have caught back up. Once you catch back up, you can continue working each problem at your normal pace.

Furthermore, don't dwell on the problems that you were rushed on. If a problem was taking up too much time and you made a hurried guess, it must be difficult. The difficult questions are the ones you are most likely to miss anyway, so it isn't a big loss. It is better to end with more time than you need than to run out of time.

Lastly, sometimes it is beneficial to slow down if you are constantly getting ahead of time. You are always more likely to catch a careless mistake by working more slowly than quickly, and among very high-scoring test takers (those who are likely to have lots of time left over), careless errors affect the score more than mastery of material.

Secret Key #2 - Guessing is not Guesswork

You probably know that guessing is a good idea. Unlike other standardized tests, there is no penalty for getting a wrong answer. Even if you have no idea about a question, you still have a 20-25% chance of getting it right.

Most test takers do not understand the impact that proper guessing can have on their score. Unless you score extremely high, guessing will significantly contribute to your final score.

Monkeys Take the Test

What most test takers don't realize is that to insure that 20-25% chance, you have to guess randomly. If you put 20 monkeys in a room to take this test, assuming they answered once per question and behaved themselves, on average they would get 20-25% of the questions correct. Put 20 test takers in the room, and the average will be much lower among guessed questions. Why?

    1. The test writers intentionally write deceptive answer choices that "look" right. A test

taker has no idea about a question, so he picks the "best looking" answer, which is often wrong. The monkey has no idea what looks good and what doesn't, so it will consistently be right about 20-25% of the time.

2. Test takers will eliminate answer choices from the guessing pool based on a hunch or intuition. Simple but correct answers often get excluded, leaving a 0% chance of being correct. The monkey has no clue, and often gets lucky with the best choice.

This is why the process of elimination endorsed by most test courses is flawed and detrimental to your performance. Test takers don't guess; they make an ignorant stab in the dark that is usually worse than random.

$5 Challenge

Let me introduce one of the most valuable ideas of this course—the $5 challenge:

You only mark your "best guess" if you are willing to bet $5 on it.
You only eliminate choices from guessing if you are willing to bet $5 on it.

Why $5? Five dollars is an amount of money that is small yet not insignificant, and can really add up fast (20 questions could cost you $100). Likewise, each answer choice on one question of the test will have a small impact on your overall score, but it can really add up to a lot of points in the end.

The process of elimination IS valuable. The following shows your chance of guessing it right:

If you eliminate wrong answer choices until only this many remain:	Chance of getting it correct:
1	100%
2	50%
3	33%

However, if you accidentally eliminate the right answer or go on a hunch for an incorrect answer, your chances drop dramatically—to 0%. By guessing among all the answer choices, you are GUARANTEED to have a shot at the right answer.

That's why the $5 test is so valuable. If you give up the advantage and safety of a pure guess, it had better be worth the risk.

What we still haven't covered is how to be sure that whatever guess you make is truly random. Here's the easiest way:

Always pick the first answer choice among those remaining.

Such a technique means that you have decided, **before you see a single test question**, exactly how you are going to guess, and since the order of choices tells you nothing about which one is correct, this guessing technique is perfectly random.

This section is not meant to scare you away from making educated guesses or eliminating choices; you just need to define when a choice is worth eliminating. The $5 test, along with a pre-defined random guessing strategy, is the best way to make sure you reap all of the benefits of guessing.

Secret Key #3 - Practice Smarter, Not Harder

Many test takers delay the test preparation process because they dread the awful amounts of practice time they think necessary to succeed on the test. We have refined an effective method that will take you only a fraction of the time.

There are a number of "obstacles" in the path to success. Among these are answering questions, finishing in time, and mastering test-taking strategies. All must be executed on the day of the test at peak performance, or your score will suffer. The test is a mental marathon that has a large impact on your future.

Just like a marathon runner, it is important to work your way up to the full challenge. So first you just worry about questions, and then time, and finally strategy:

Success Strategy

1. Find a good source for practice tests.
2. If you are willing to make a larger time investment, consider using more than one study guide. Often the different approaches of multiple authors will help you "get" difficult concepts.
3. Take a practice test with no time constraints, with all study helps, "open book." Take your time with questions and focus on applying strategies.
4. Take a practice test with time constraints, with all guides, "open book."
5. Take a final practice test without open material and with time limits.

If you have time to take more practice tests, just repeat step 5. By gradually exposing yourself to the full rigors of the test environment, you will condition your mind to the stress of test day and maximize your success.

Secret Key #4 - Prepare, Don't Procrastinate

Let me state an obvious fact: if you take the test three times, you will probably get three different scores. This is due to the way you feel on test day, the level of preparedness you have, and the version of the test you see. Despite the test writers' claims to the contrary, some versions of the test WILL be easier for you than others.

Since your future depends so much on your score, you should maximize your chances of success. In order to maximize the likelihood of success, you've got to prepare in advance. This means taking practice tests and spending time learning the information and test taking strategies you will need to succeed.

Never go take the actual test as a "practice" test, expecting that you can just take it again if you need to. Take all the practice tests you can on your own, but when you go to take the official test, be prepared, be focused, and do your best the first time!

Secret Key #5 - Test Yourself

Everyone knows that time is money. There is no need to spend too much of your time or too little of your time preparing for the test. You should only spend as much of your precious time preparing as is necessary for you to get the score you need.

Once you have taken a practice test under real conditions of time constraints, then you will know if you are ready for the test or not.

If you have scored extremely high the first time that you take the practice test, then there is not much point in spending countless hours studying. You are already there.

Benchmark your abilities by retaking practice tests and seeing how much you have improved. Once you consistently score high enough to guarantee success, then you are ready.

If you have scored well below where you need, then knuckle down and begin studying in earnest. Check your improvement regularly through the use of practice tests under real conditions. Above all, don't worry, panic, or give up. The key is perseverance!

Then, when you go to take the test, remain confident and remember how well you did on the practice tests. If you can score high enough on a practice test, then you can do the same on the real thing.

General Strategies

The most important thing you can do is to ignore your fears and jump into the test immediately. Do not be overwhelmed by any strange-sounding terms. You have to jump into the test like jumping into a pool—all at once is the easiest way.

Make Predictions

As you read and understand the question, try to guess what the answer will be. Remember that several of the answer choices are wrong, and once you begin reading them, your mind will immediately become cluttered with answer choices designed to throw you off. Your mind is typically the most focused immediately after you have read the question and digested its contents. If you can, try to predict what the correct answer will be. You may be surprised at what you can predict.

Quickly scan the choices and see if your prediction is in the listed answer choices. If it is, then you can be quite confident that you have the right answer. It still won't hurt to check the other answer choices, but most of the time, you've got it!

Answer the Question

It may seem obvious to only pick answer choices that answer the question, but the test writers can create some excellent answer choices that are wrong. Don't pick an answer just because it sounds right, or you believe it to be true. It MUST answer the question. Once you've made your selection, always go back and check it against the question and make sure that you didn't misread the question and that the answer choice does answer the question posed.

Benchmark

After you read the first answer choice, decide if you think it sounds correct or not. If it doesn't, move on to the next answer choice. If it does, mentally mark that answer choice. This doesn't mean that you've definitely selected it as your answer choice, it just means that it's the best you've seen thus far. Go ahead and read the next choice. If the next choice is worse than the one you've already selected, keep going to the next answer choice. If the next choice is better than the choice you've already selected, mentally mark the new answer choice as your best guess.

The first answer choice that you select becomes your standard. Every other answer choice must be benchmarked against that standard. That choice is correct until proven otherwise by another answer choice beating it out. Once you've decided that no other answer choice seems as good, do one final check to ensure that your answer choice answers the question posed.

Valid Information

Don't discount any of the information provided in the question. Every piece of information may be necessary to determine the correct answer. None of the information in the question is there to throw you off (while the answer choices will certainly have information to throw you off). If two seemingly unrelated topics are discussed, don't ignore either. You can be confident there is a relationship, or it wouldn't be included in the question, and you are probably going to have to determine what is that relationship to find the answer.

Avoid "Fact Traps"

Don't get distracted by a choice that is factually true. Your search is for the answer that answers the question. Stay focused and don't fall for an answer that is true but irrelevant. Always go back to the question and make sure you're choosing an answer that actually answers the question and is not just a true statement. An answer can be factually correct, but it MUST answer the question asked. Additionally, two answers can both be seemingly correct, so be sure to read all of the answer choices, and make sure that you get the one that BEST answers the question.

Milk the Question

Some of the questions may throw you completely off. They might deal with a subject you have not been exposed to, or one that you haven't reviewed in years. While your lack of knowledge about the subject will be a hindrance, the question itself can give you many clues that will help you find the correct answer. Read the question carefully and look for clues. Watch particularly for adjectives and nouns describing difficult terms or words that you don't recognize. Regardless of whether you completely understand a word or not, replacing it with a synonym, either provided or one you more familiar with, may help you to understand what the questions are asking. Rather than wracking your mind about specific detailed information concerning a difficult term or word, try to use mental substitutes that are easier to understand.

The Trap of Familiarity

Don't just choose a word because you recognize it. On difficult questions, you may not recognize a number of words in the answer choices. The test writers don't put "make-believe" words on the test, so don't think that just because you only recognize all the words in one answer choice that that answer choice must be correct. If you only recognize words in one answer choice, then focus on that one. Is it correct? Try your best to determine if it is correct. If it is, that's great. If not, eliminate it. Each word and answer choice you eliminate increases your chances of getting the question correct, even if you then have to guess among the unfamiliar choices.

Eliminate Answers

Eliminate choices as soon as you realize they are wrong. But be careful! Make sure you consider all of the possible answer choices. Just because one appears right, doesn't mean that the next one won't be even better! The test writers will usually put more than one good answer choice for every question, so read all of them. Don't worry if you are stuck between two that seem right. By getting down to just two remaining possible choices, your odds are now 50/50. Rather than wasting too much time, play the odds. You are guessing, but guessing wisely because you've been able to knock out some of the answer choices that you know are wrong. If you are eliminating choices and realize that the last answer choice you are left with is also obviously wrong, don't panic. Start over and consider each choice again. There may easily be something that you missed the first time and will realize on the second pass.

Tough Questions

If you are stumped on a problem or it appears too hard or too difficult, don't waste time. Move on! Remember though, if you can quickly check for obviously incorrect answer choices, your chances of guessing correctly are greatly improved. Before you completely give up, at least try to knock out a couple of possible answers. Eliminate what you can and then guess at the remaining answer choices before moving on.

Brainstorm

If you get stuck on a difficult question, spend a few seconds quickly brainstorming. Run through the complete list of possible answer choices. Look at each choice and ask yourself, "Could this answer the question satisfactorily?" Go through each answer choice and consider it independently of the others. By systematically going through all possibilities, you may find something that you would otherwise overlook. Remember though that when you get stuck, it's important to try to keep moving.

Read Carefully

Understand the problem. Read the question and answer choices carefully. Don't miss the question because you misread the terms. You have plenty of time to read each question thoroughly and make sure you understand what is being asked. Yet a happy medium must be attained, so don't waste too much time. You must read carefully, but efficiently.

Face Value

When in doubt, use common sense. Always accept the situation in the problem at face value. Don't read too much into it. These problems will not require you to make huge leaps of logic. The test writers aren't trying to throw you off with a cheap trick. If you have to go beyond creativity and make a leap of logic in order to have an answer choice answer the question, then you should look at the other answer choices. Don't overcomplicate the problem by creating theoretical relationships or explanations that will warp time or space. These are normal problems rooted in reality. It's just that the applicable relationship or explanation may not be readily apparent and you have to figure things out. Use your common sense to interpret anything that isn't clear.

Prefixes

If you're having trouble with a word in the question or answer choices, try dissecting it. Take advantage of every clue that the word might include. Prefixes and suffixes can be a huge help. Usually they allow you to determine a basic meaning. Pre- means before, post- means after, pro - is positive, de- is negative. From these prefixes and suffixes, you can get an idea of the general meaning of the word and try to put it into context. Beware though of any traps. Just because con- is the opposite of pro-, doesn't necessarily mean congress is the opposite of progress!

Hedge Phrases

Watch out for critical hedge phrases, led off with words such as "likely," "may," "can," "sometimes," "often," "almost," "mostly," "usually," "generally," "rarely," and "sometimes." Question writers insert these hedge phrases to cover every possibility. Often an answer choice will be wrong simply because it leaves no room for exception. Unless the situation calls for them, avoid answer choices that have definitive words like "exactly," and "always."

Switchback Words

Stay alert for "switchbacks." These are the words and phrases frequently used to alert you to shifts in thought. The most common switchback word is "but." Others include "although," "however," "nevertheless," "on the other hand," "even though," "while," "in spite of," "despite," and "regardless of."

New Information

Correct answer choices will rarely have completely new information included. Answer choices typically are straightforward reflections of the material asked about and will directly relate to the question. If a new piece of information is included in an answer choice that doesn't even seem to relate to the topic being asked about, then that answer choice is likely incorrect. All of the information needed to answer the question is usually provided for you in the question. You should not have to make guesses that are unsupported or choose answer choices that require unknown information that cannot be reasoned from what is given.

Time Management

On technical questions, don't get lost on the technical terms. Don't spend too much time on any one question. If you don't know what a term means, then odds are you aren't going to get much further since you don't have a dictionary. You should be able to immediately recognize whether or not you know a term. If you don't, work with the other clues that you have—the other answer choices and terms provided—but don't waste too much time trying to figure out a difficult term that you don't know.

Contextual Clues

Look for contextual clues. An answer can be right but not the correct answer. The contextual clues will help you find the answer that is most right and is correct. Understand the context in which a phrase or statement is made. This will help you make important distinctions.

Don't Panic

Panicking will not answer any questions for you; therefore, it isn't helpful. When you first see the question, if your mind goes blank, take a deep breath. Force yourself to mechanically go through the steps of solving the problem using the strategies you've learned.

Pace Yourself

Don't get clock fever. It's easy to be overwhelmed when you're looking at a page full of questions, your mind is full of random thoughts and feeling confused, and the clock is ticking down faster than you would like. Calm down and maintain the pace that you have set for yourself. As long as you are on track by monitoring your pace, you are guaranteed to have enough time for yourself. When you get to the last few minutes of the test, it may seem like you won't have enough time left, but if you only have as many questions as you should have left at that point, then you're right on track!

Answer Selection

The best way to pick an answer choice is to eliminate all of those that are wrong, until only one is left and confirm that is the correct answer. Sometimes though, an answer choice may immediately look right. Be careful! Take a second to make sure that the other choices are not equally obvious. Don't make a hasty mistake. There are only two times that you should stop before checking other answers. First is when you are positive that the answer choice you have selected is correct. Second is when time is almost out and you have to make a quick guess!

Check Your Work

Since you will probably not know every term listed and the answer to every question, it is important that you get credit for the ones that you do know. Don't miss any questions through careless mistakes. If at all possible, try to take a second to look back over your answer selection and make sure you've selected the correct answer choice and haven't made a costly careless mistake (such as marking an answer choice that you didn't mean to mark). The time it takes for this quick double check should more than pay for itself in caught mistakes.

Beware of Directly Quoted Answers

Sometimes an answer choice will repeat word for word a portion of the question or reference section. However, beware of such exact duplication. It may be a trap! More than likely, the correct choice will paraphrase or summarize a point, rather than being exactly the same wording.

Slang

Scientific sounding answers are better than slang ones. An answer choice that begins "To compare the outcomes..." is much more likely to be correct than one that begins "Because some people insisted..."

Extreme Statements

Avoid wild answers that throw out highly controversial ideas that are proclaimed as established fact. An answer choice that states the "process should used in certain situations, if..." is much more likely to be correct than one that states the "process should be discontinued completely."   The first is a calm rational statement and doesn't even make a definitive, uncompromising stance, using a hedge word "if" to provide wiggle room, whereas the second choice is a radical idea and far more extreme.

Answer Choice Families

When you have two or more answer choices that are direct opposites or parallels, one of them is usually the correct answer. For instance, if one answer choice states "x increases" and another answer choice states "x decreases" or "y increases," then those two or three answer choices are very similar in construction and fall into the same family of answer choices. A family of answer choices consists of two or three answer choices, very similar in construction, but often with directly opposite meanings.   Usually the correct answer choice will be in that family of answer choices. The "odd man out" or answer choice that doesn't seem to fit the parallel construction of the other answer choices is more likely to be incorrect.

Special Report: What is Test Anxiety and How to Overcome It?

The very nature of tests caters to some level of anxiety, nervousness, or tension, just as we feel for any important event that occurs in our lives. A little bit of anxiety or nervousness can be a good thing. It helps us with motivation, and makes achievement just that much sweeter. However, too much anxiety can be a problem, especially if it hinders our ability to function and perform.

"Test anxiety," is the term that refers to the emotional reactions that some test-takers experience when faced with a test or exam. Having a fear of testing and exams is based upon a rational fear, since the test-taker's performance can shape the course of an academic career. Nevertheless, experiencing excessive fear of examinations will only interfere with the test-taker's ability to perform and chance to be successful.

There are a large variety of causes that can contribute to the development and sensation of test anxiety. These include, but are not limited to, lack of preparation and worrying about issues surrounding the test.

Lack of Preparation

Lack of preparation can be identified by the following behaviors or situations:

Not scheduling enough time to study, and therefore cramming the night before the test or exam
Managing time poorly, to create the sensation that there is not enough time to do everything
Failing to organize the text information in advance, so that the study material consists of the entire text and not simply the pertinent information
Poor overall studying habits

Worrying, on the other hand, can be related to both the test taker, or many other factors around him/her that will be affected by the results of the test. These include worrying about:

Previous performances on similar exams, or exams in general
How friends and other students are achieving
The negative consequences that will result from a poor grade or failure

There are three primary elements to test anxiety. Physical components, which involve the same typical bodily reactions as those to acute anxiety (to be discussed below). Emotional factors have to do with fear or panic. Mental or cognitive issues concerning attention spans and memory abilities.

Physical Signals

There are many different symptoms of test anxiety, and these are not limited to mental and emotional strain. Frequently there are a range of physical signals that will let a test taker know that he/she is suffering from test anxiety. These bodily changes can include the following:

Perspiring
Sweaty palms
Wet, trembling hands
Nausea
Dry mouth
A knot in the stomach
Headache
Faintness
Muscle tension
Aching shoulders, back and neck
Rapid heart beat
Feeling too hot/cold

To recognize the sensation of test anxiety, a test-taker should monitor him/herself for the following sensations:

The physical distress symptoms as listed above
Emotional sensitivity, expressing emotional feelings such as the need to cry or laugh too much, or a sensation of anger or helplessness
A decreased ability to think, causing the test-taker to blank out or have racing thoughts that are hard to organize or control.

Though most students will feel some level of anxiety when faced with a test or exam, the majority can cope with that anxiety and maintain it at a manageable level. However, those who cannot are faced with a very real and very serious condition, which can and should be controlled for the immeasurable benefit of this sufferer.

Naturally, these sensations lead to negative results for the testing experience. The most common effects of test anxiety have to do with nervousness and mental blocking.

Nervousness

Nervousness can appear in several different levels:

The test-taker's difficulty, or even inability to read and understand the questions on the test
The difficulty or inability to organize thoughts to a coherent form
The difficulty or inability to recall key words and concepts relating to the testing questions (especially essays)
The receipt of poor grades on a test, though the test material was well known by the test taker

Conversely, a person may also experience mental blocking, which involves:

Blanking out on test questions
Only remembering the correct answers to the questions when the test has already finished.

Fortunately for test anxiety sufferers, beating these feelings, to a large degree, has to do with proper preparation. When a test taker has a feeling of preparedness, then anxiety will be dramatically lessened.

The first step to resolving anxiety issues is to distinguish which of the two types of anxiety are being suffered. If the anxiety is a direct result of a lack of preparation, this should be considered a normal reaction, and the anxiety level (as opposed to the test results) shouldn't be anything to worry about. However, if, when adequately prepared, the test-taker still panics, blanks out, or seems to overreact, this is not a fully rational reaction. While this can be considered normal too, there are many ways to combat and overcome these effects.

Remember that anxiety cannot be entirely eliminated, however, there are ways to minimize it, to make the anxiety easier to manage. Preparation is one of the best ways to minimize test anxiety. Therefore the following techniques are wise in order to best fight off any anxiety that may want to build.

To begin with, try to avoid cramming before a test, whenever it is possible. By trying to memorize an entire term's worth of information in one day, you'll be shocking your system, and not giving yourself a very good chance to absorb the information. This is an easy path to anxiety, so for those who suffer from test anxiety, cramming should not even be considered an option.

Instead of cramming, work throughout the semester to combine all of the material which is presented throughout the semester, and work on it gradually as the course goes by, making sure to master the main concepts first, leaving minor details for a week or so before the test.

To study for the upcoming exam, be sure to pose questions that may be on the examination, to gauge the ability to answer them by integrating the ideas from your texts, notes and lectures, as well as any supplementary readings.

If it is truly impossible to cover all of the information that was covered in that particular term, concentrate on the most important portions, that can be covered very well. Learn these concepts as best as possible, so that when the test comes, a goal can be made to use these concepts as presentations of your knowledge.

In addition to study habits, changes in attitude are critical to beating a struggle with test anxiety. In fact, an improvement of the perspective over the entire test-taking experience can actually help a test taker to enjoy studying and therefore improve the overall experience. Be certain not to overemphasize the significance of the grade - know that the result of the test is neither a reflection of self worth, nor is it a measure of intelligence; one grade will not predict a person's future success.

To improve an overall testing outlook, the following steps should be tried:

Keeping in mind that the most reasonable expectation for taking a test is to expect to try to demonstrate as much of what you know as you possibly can.
Reminding ourselves that a test is only one test; this is not the only one, and there will be others.
The thought of thinking of oneself in an irrational, all-or-nothing term should be avoided at all costs.
A reward should be designated for after the test, so there's something to look forward to. Whether it be going to a movie, going out to eat, or simply visiting friends, schedule it in advance, and do it no matter what result is expected on the exam.

Test-takers should also keep in mind that the basics are some of the most important things, even beyond anti-anxiety techniques and studying. Never neglect the basic social, emotional and biological needs, in order to try to absorb information. In order to best achieve, these three factors must be held as just as important as the studying itself.

Study Steps

Remember the following important steps for studying:

Maintain healthy nutrition and exercise habits. Continue both your recreational activities and social pass times. These both contribute to your physical and emotional well being.
Be certain to get a good amount of sleep, especially the night before the test, because when you're overtired you are not able to perform to the best of your best ability.
Keep the studying pace to a moderate level by taking breaks when they are needed, and varying the work whenever possible, to keep the mind fresh instead of getting bored. When enough studying has been done that all the material that can be learned has been learned, and the test taker is prepared for the test, stop studying and do something relaxing such as listening to music, watching a movie, or taking a warm bubble bath.

There are also many other techniques to minimize the uneasiness or apprehension that is experienced along with test anxiety before, during, or even after the examination. In fact, there are a great deal of things that can be done to stop anxiety from interfering with lifestyle and performance. Again, remember that anxiety will not be eliminated entirely, and it shouldn't be. Otherwise that "up" feeling for exams would not exist, and most of us depend on that sensation to perform better than usual. However, this anxiety has to be at a level that is manageable.

Of course, as we have just discussed, being prepared for the exam is half the battle right away. Attending all classes, finding out what knowledge will be expected on the exam, and knowing the exam schedules are easy steps to lowering anxiety. Keeping up with work will remove the need to cram, and efficient study habits will eliminate wasted time. Studying should be done in an ideal location for concentration, so that it is simple to become interested in the material and give it complete attention. A method such as SQ3R (Survey, Question, Read, Recite, Review) is a wonderful key to follow to make sure that the study habits are as effective as possible, especially in the case of learning from a textbook. Flashcards are great techniques for memorization. Learning to take good notes will mean that notes will be full of useful information, so that less sifting will need to be done to seek out what is pertinent for studying. Reviewing notes after class and then again on occasion will keep the information fresh in the mind. From notes that have been taken summary sheets and outlines can be made for simpler reviewing.

A study group can also be a very motivational and helpful place to study, as there will be a sharing of ideas, all of the minds can work together, to make sure that everyone understands, and the studying will be made more interesting because it will be a social occasion.

Basically, though, as long as the test-taker remains organized and self confident, with efficient study habits, less time will need to be spent studying, and higher grades will be achieved.

To become self confident, there are many useful steps. The first of these is "self talk." It has been shown through extensive research, that self-talk for students who suffer from test anxiety, should be well monitored, in order to make sure that it contributes to self confidence as opposed to sinking the student. Frequently the self talk of test-anxious students is negative or self-defeating, thinking that everyone else is smarter and faster, that they always mess up, and that if they don't do well, they'll fail the entire course. It is important to decreasing anxiety that awareness is made of self talk. Try writing any negative self thoughts and then disputing them with a positive statement instead. Begin self-encouragement as though it was a friend speaking. Repeat positive statements to help reprogram the mind to believing in successes instead of failures.

Helpful Techniques

Other extremely helpful techniques include:

Self-visualization of doing well and reaching goals
While aiming for an "A" level of understanding, don't try to "overprotect" by setting your expectations lower. This will only convince the mind to stop studying in order to meet the lower expectations.
Don't make comparisons with the results or habits of other students. These are individual factors, and different things work for different people, causing different results.
Strive to become an expert in learning what works well, and what can be done in order to improve. Consider collecting this data in a journal.
Create rewards for after studying instead of doing things before studying that will only turn into avoidance behaviors.
Make a practice of relaxing - by using methods such as progressive relaxation, self-hypnosis, guided imagery, etc - in order to make relaxation an automatic sensation.
Work on creating a state of relaxed concentration so that concentrating will take on the focus of the mind, so that none will be wasted on worrying.
Take good care of the physical self by eating well and getting enough sleep.
Plan in time for exercise and stick to this plan.

Beyond these techniques, there are other methods to be used before, during and after the test that will help the test-taker perform well in addition to overcoming anxiety.

Before the exam comes the academic preparation. This involves establishing a study schedule and beginning at least one week before the actual date of the test. By doing this, the anxiety of not having enough time to study for the test will be automatically eliminated. Moreover, this will make the studying a much more effective experience, ensuring that the learning will be an easier process. This relieves much undue pressure on the test-taker.

Summary sheets, note cards, and flash cards with the main concepts and examples of these main concepts should be prepared in advance of the actual studying time. A topic should never be eliminated from this process. By omitting a topic because it isn't expected to be on the test is only setting up the test-taker for anxiety should it actually appear on the exam. Utilize the course syllabus for laying out the topics that should be studied. Carefully go over the notes that were made in class, paying special attention to any of the issues that the professor took special care to emphasize while lecturing in class. In the textbooks, use the chapter review, or if possible, the chapter tests, to begin your review.

It may even be possible to ask the instructor what information will be covered on the exam, or what the format of the exam will be (for example, multiple choice, essay, free form, true-false). Additionally, see if it is possible to find out how many questions will be on the test. If a review sheet or sample test has been offered by the professor, make good use of it, above anything else, for the preparation for the test. Another great resource for getting to know the examination is reviewing tests from previous semesters. Use these tests to review, and aim to achieve a 100% score on each of the possible topics. With a few exceptions, the goal that you set for yourself is the highest one that you will reach.

Take all of the questions that were assigned as homework, and rework them to any other possible course material. The more problems reworked, the more skill and confidence will form as a result. When forming the solution to a problem, write out each of the steps. Don't simply do head work. By doing as many steps on paper as possible, much clarification and therefore confidence will be formed. Do this with as many homework problems as possible, before checking the answers. By checking the answer after each problem, a reinforcement will exist, that will not be on the exam. Study situations should be as exam-like as possible, to prime the test-taker's system for the experience. By waiting to check the answers at the end, a psychological advantage will be formed, to decrease the stress factor.

Another fantastic reason for not cramming is the avoidance of confusion in concepts, especially when it comes to mathematics. 8-10 hours of study will become one hundred percent more effective if it is spread out over a week or at least several days, instead of doing it all in one sitting. Recognize that the human brain requires time in order to assimilate new material, so frequent breaks and a span of study time over several days will be much more beneficial.

Additionally, don't study right up until the point of the exam. Studying should stop a minimum of one hour before the exam begins. This allows the brain to rest and put things in their proper order. This will also provide the time to become as relaxed as possible when going into the examination room. The test-taker will also have time to eat well and eat sensibly. Know that the brain needs food as much as the rest of the body. With enough food and enough sleep, as well as a relaxed attitude, the body and the mind are primed for success.

Avoid any anxious classmates who are talking about the exam. These students only spread anxiety, and are not worth sharing the anxious sentimentalities.

Before the test also involves creating a positive attitude, so mental preparation should also be a point of concentration. There are many keys to creating a positive attitude. Should fears become rushing in, make a visualization of taking the exam, doing well, and seeing an A written on the paper. Write out a list of affirmations that will bring a feeling of confidence, such as "I am doing well in my English class," "I studied well and know my material," "I enjoy this class." Even if the affirmations aren't believed at first, it sends a positive message to the subconscious which will result in an alteration of the overall belief system, which is the system that creates reality.

If a sensation of panic begins, work with the fear and imagine the very worst! Work through the entire scenario of not passing the test, failing the entire course, and dropping out of school, followed by not getting a job, and pushing a shopping cart through the dark alley where you'll live. This will place things into perspective! Then, practice deep breathing and create a visualization of the opposite situation - achieving an "A" on the exam, passing the entire course, receiving the degree at a graduation ceremony.

On the day of the test, there are many things to be done to ensure the best results, as well as the most calm outlook. The following stages are suggested in order to maximize test-taking potential:

Begin the examination day with a moderate breakfast, and avoid any coffee or beverages with caffeine if the test taker is prone to jitters. Even people who are used to managing caffeine can feel jittery or light-headed when it is taken on a test day.
Attempt to do something that is relaxing before the examination begins. As last minute cramming clouds the mastering of overall concepts, it is better to use this time to create a calming outlook.
Be certain to arrive at the test location well in advance, in order to provide time to select a location that is away from doors, windows and other distractions, as well as giving enough time to relax before the test begins.
Keep away from anxiety generating classmates who will upset the sensation of stability and relaxation that is being attempted before the exam.
Should the waiting period before the exam begins cause anxiety, create a self-distraction by reading a light magazine or something else that is relaxing and simple.

During the exam itself, read the entire exam from beginning to end, and find out how much time should be allotted to each individual problem. Once writing the exam, should more time be taken for a problem, it should be abandoned, in order to begin another problem. If there is time at the end, the unfinished problem can always be returned to and completed.

Read the instructions very carefully - twice - so that unpleasant surprises won't follow during or after the exam has ended.

When writing the exam, pretend that the situation is actually simply the completion of homework within a library, or at home. This will assist in forming a relaxed atmosphere, and will allow the brain extra focus for the complex thinking function.

Begin the exam with all of the questions with which the most confidence is felt. This will build the confidence level regarding the entire exam and will begin a quality momentum. This will also create encouragement for trying the problems where uncertainty resides.

Going with the "gut instinct" is always the way to go when solving a problem. Second guessing should be avoided at all costs. Have confidence in the ability to do well.

For essay questions, create an outline in advance that will keep the mind organized and make certain that all of the points are remembered. For multiple choice, read every answer, even if the correct one has been spotted - a better one may exist.

Continue at a pace that is reasonable and not rushed, in order to be able to work carefully. Provide enough time to go over the answers at the end, to check for small errors that can be corrected.

Should a feeling of panic begin, breathe deeply, and think of the feeling of the body releasing sand through its pores. Visualize a calm, peaceful place, and include all of the sights, sounds and sensations of this image. Continue the deep breathing, and take a few minutes to continue this with closed eyes. When all is well again, return to the test.

If a "blanking" occurs for a certain question, skip it and move on to the next question. There will be time to return to the other question later. Get everything done that can be done, first, to guarantee all the grades that can be compiled, and to build all of the confidence possible. Then return to the weaker questions to build the marks from there.

Remember, one's own reality can be created, so as long as the belief is there, success will follow. And remember: anxiety can happen later, right now, there's an exam to be written!

After the examination is complete, whether there is a feeling for a good grade or a bad grade, don't dwell on the exam, and be certain to follow through on the reward that was promised...and enjoy it! Don't dwell on any mistakes that have been made, as there is nothing that can be done at this point anyway.

Additionally, don't begin to study for the next test right away. Do something relaxing for a while, and let the mind relax and prepare itself to begin absorbing information again.

From the results of the exam - both the grade and the entire experience, be certain to learn from what has gone on. Perfect studying habits and work some more on confidence in order to make the next examination experience even better than the last one.

Learn to avoid places where openings occurred for laziness, procrastination and day dreaming.

Use the time between this exam and the next one to better learn to relax, even learning to relax on cue, so that any anxiety can be controlled during the next exam. Learn how to relax the body. Slouch in your chair if that helps. Tighten and then relax all of the different muscle groups, one group at a time, beginning with the feet and then working all the way up to the neck and face. This will ultimately relax the muscles more than they were to begin with. Learn how to breathe deeply and comfortably, and focus on this breathing going in and out as a relaxing thought. With every exhale, repeat the word "relax."

As common as test anxiety is, it is very possible to overcome it. Make yourself one of the test-takers who overcome this frustrating hindrance.

Special Report: Retaking the Test: What Are Your Chances at Improving Your Score?

After going through the experience of taking a major test, many test takers feel that once is enough. The test usually comes during a period of transition in the test taker's life, and taking the test is only one of a series of important events. With so many distractions and conflicting recommendations, it may be difficult for a test taker to rationally determine whether or not he should retake the test after viewing his scores.

The importance of the test usually only adds to the burden of the retake decision. However, don't be swayed by emotion. There a few simple questions that you can ask yourself to guide you as you try to determine whether a retake would improve your score:

1. What went wrong? Why wasn't your score what you expected?

Can you point to a single factor or problem that you feel caused the low score? Were you sick on test day? Was there an emotional upheaval in your life that caused a distraction? Were you late for the test or not able to use the full time allotment? If you can point to any of these specific, individual problems, then a retake should definitely be considered.

2. Is there enough time to improve?

Many problems that may show up in your score report may take a lot of time for improvement. A deficiency in a particular math skill may require weeks or months of tutoring and studying to improve. If you have enough time to improve an identified weakness, then a retake should definitely be considered.

3. How will additional scores be used? Will a score average, highest score, or most recent score be used?

Different test scores may be handled completely differently. If you've taken the test multiple times, sometimes your highest score is used, sometimes your average score is computed and used, and sometimes your most recent score is used. Make sure you understand what method will be used to evaluate your scores, and use that to help you determine whether a retake should be considered.

4. Are my practice test scores significantly higher than my actual test score?

If you have taken a lot of practice tests and are consistently scoring at a much higher level than your actual test score, then you should consider a retake. However, if you've taken five practice tests and only one of your scores was higher than your actual test score, or if your practice test scores were only slightly higher than your actual test score, then it is unlikely that you will significantly increase your score.

5. Do I need perfect scores or will I be able to live with this score? Will this score still allow me to follow my dreams?

What kind of score is acceptable to you? Is your current score "good enough?" Do you have to have a certain score in order to pursue the future of your dreams? If you won't be happy with your current score, and there's no way that you could live with it, then you should consider a retake. However, don't get your hopes up. If you are looking for significant improvement, that may or may not be possible. But if you won't be happy otherwise, it is at least worth the effort.
Remember that there are other considerations. To achieve your dream, it is likely that your grades may also be taken into account. A great test score is usually not the only thing necessary to succeed. Make sure that you aren't overemphasizing the importance of a high test score.

Furthermore, a retake does not always result in a higher score. Some test takers will score lower on a retake, rather than higher. One study shows that one-fourth of test takers will achieve a significant improvement in test score, while one-sixth of test takers will actually show a decrease. While this shows that most test takers will improve, the majority will only improve their scores a little and a retake may not be worth the test taker's effort.

Finally, if a test is taken only once and is considered in the added context of good grades on the part of a test taker, the person reviewing the grades and scores may be tempted to assume that the test taker just had a bad day while taking the test, and may discount the low test score in favor of the high grades. But if the test is retaken and the scores are approximately the same, then the validity of the low scores are only confirmed. Therefore, a retake could actually hurt a test taker by definitely bracketing a test taker's score ability to a limited range.

Special Report: Additional Bonus Material

Due to our efforts to try to keep this book to a manageable length, we've created a link that will give you access to all of your additional bonus material.

Please visit http://www.mometrix.com/bonus948/sixsigmabb to access the information.